# MAYOR:
## Notes on the Sixties

by
# IVAN ALLEN, JR.,
former Mayor of Atlanta,

with PAUL HEMPHILL

SIMON AND SCHUSTER | NEW YORK

To my father, who saw it coming;
and to my wife, whose advice and
courage saw me through it

Copyright © 1971 by Ivan Allen, Jr., and Paul Hemphill
Published by Simon and Schuster
Rockefeller Center, 630 Fifth Avenue
New York, New York 10020

First Printing

SBN 671-20889-6

Library of Congress Catalog Card Number: 76-139627
Designed by Edith Fowler
Manufactured in the United States of America

# Contents

# Foreword

The cities are where the action is. And that's where Ivan Allen was throughout the 1960's. Whenever there was a fight for the future of Atlanta or the rights of people, Mayor Allen was in the middle of it. He spoke up for civil rights long before commentators heralded the rise of a moderate "new South." He worked for sensible national priorities long before most officials realized that American cities and urban citizens were in trouble. In Atlanta and in Georgia, in his region and in the country, he was a leader who refused to follow the myths and prejudices of the past. He risked political failure—and built a record of remarkable public success.

Today, you can see Mayor Allen's success in the physical renaissance of Atlanta—in the revived neighborhoods, the new stadium, the booming business on Peachtree Street. What cannot be seen—though a visitor can almost feel it—is the sense of pride and confidence Ivan Allen gave to Atlanta. He challenged Atlantans to live up to what was best in their heritage—and they responded.

This book is the story of his challenge and their response. It is literate, exciting, and fascinating—and it is more than an enjoyable night's reading. The story Mayor

Allen tells here also conveys vital lessons about governing a modern American city. The Mayor brought to City Hall just the right combination of qualities. He was idealistic and pragmatic, visionary and practical—a professional in every good sense of the word. And he used those qualities to reshape and renew his city.

That is no small accomplishment in a country where cities face a constant crisis of survival; where Washington spends more money on war than on people; where, each year, mayors must struggle to finance *absolutely* increasing demands with *relatively* less and less revenue. Ivan Allen tried to change all that, at home and across America. He left behind him a tradition of commitment and competence. His able and courageous successor in Atlanta, Sam Massell, is typical of the mayors who are now working in Ivan Allen's tradition.

Mayor Allen no longer sits in Atlanta's City Hall. But few Atlantans will forget what he did while he was there. When the history of urban America in our time is written, Ivan Allen will be singled out for the kind of praise few mayors have earned. Of him, it will be accurately said that he made a very real difference.

*March 2, 1971*                                       John V. Lindsay

# Prologue

---

My generation has completely failed in every way to enlighten or solve the major issue which our section of the country has, the race issue . . . Your generation is going to be confronted with it, and it will be the greatest agony that any generation ever went through . . .

—My father, to me, in 1947

Few people would argue that racial equality has yet been accomplished in the South, or anywhere else in the United States, but the racial progress that *has* been made seems incredible when you go back and look at the situation as it stood at the end of World War II. The Southern Way of Life still ruled then. Total segregation and subjugation of the Negro was a reality that was seldom questioned, even by the Negro himself. The Negro was allowed to spend his money in the white man's stores, but he rode downtown in the back of the trolley and when he got there was not permitted to eat in the same restaurant or use the same restroom as the white man. The Negro lived in "nigger-town," drank from a COLORED water fountain, sat in the "nigger bleachers" at the ballpark and the most distant balcony at the movie house, attended a separate-and-unequal school, worked as a laborer or a maid, ordered his food from the back door, and looked the other way while the white man howled with laughter at a black-face comedy routine. There was no one, in those days, to speak for the black man. "Liberal" is a relative word, and a liberal on the race issue in the South during the forties was some-one—and I don't think this is overstating it too much—who felt vaguely uncomfortable over the mistreatment of people with black skin. That was the system, though, and the thought of challenging it occurred to few Southerners in those days.

The saddest fact of the matter was, the South had so segregated itself for so long that there were virtually no lines of communication between the races. Few of us who were raised in the South during the first half of the twentieth century can honestly say we knew any black people well enough to truly appreciate what it was like for them, in spite of the fact that the majority of black Americans lived in our part of the country. They were there—as our maids, as our yard men, as our street sweepers—but we never actually *saw* them.

My background was fairly typical. My father was raised near Chattanooga in a town called Dalton, in northern Georgia, where some counties still boast of having not a single Negro resident. He came to Atlanta in 1895 as a twenty-year-old typewriter salesman, struggled for a while, then established an office equipment firm known now as the Ivan Allen Company. I was born in a rambling frame house on West Peachtree Street in 1911, and because the doctor was unable to make it in time for the birthing a

Negro woman named Bertha Lewis attended my mother as midwife. But after that first moment of my life, when the first hand to touch me was a black hand, it was a very long time before I came into close personal contact with a Negro again—except with the succession of maids who helped raise me and, later, raise my own children. We were members of the comfortable white Southern business establishment, and therefore had no reason to mingle with the black except on a paternalistic boss-to-lackey basis. There was a time when a friend of mine and I were challenged to a golf match by two young Negroes who worked around the pro shop at the Capital City Country Club: the club pro finally relented to the match, but said we would have to play at 4 o'clock on a Monday morning, and there were 250 caddies rooting for the two Negroes and only my friend's father rooting for us. The fact that because this was a biracial match we had to play at dawn stirred me a little, but not enough to make a lasting impression, and I honestly can't recall that the racial issue was ever even mentioned while I was a student at Georgia Tech. Even those of us who later were to admire Franklin Delano Roosevelt, my father and myself included, tended to think of poor whites in the rural South when we heard the term "social problems." We had only the vague feeling that the Negro's lot was not good. But, then, that was the system.

It was not until 1947, when I was thirty-six, that I had my first awakening to the problems of the Negro. That year I was selected to head the Community Chest fund drive, traditionally one of the first civic projects in which an up-and-coming young businessman in Atlanta becomes involved. I was extremely young, and the job was far too big for me—the Community Chest had gone through some rather unsuccessful campaigns during the last part of the war, and there was a great need for a successful one this time around—but I was one of those being chosen to eventually take over the leadership of the city and so the job was thrown to me. Anyway, even in a charity such as the Community Chest fund drive there was a shadow of bigotry. In making up the budget for that year the white leadership of the Community Chest went into deep discussion over an allocation of $500 that was to go to the Atlanta Urban League to take care of the national dues of the local director, Grace Hamilton, a superb Negro lady whose husband was registrar of Atlanta University. The Urban League may be regarded as a conservative organization now, more than twenty years later, but it struck fear in the hearts of Southern whites then. Using the argument that Mrs. Hamilton's $500 eventually would be used for Communist purposes, to organize Negro rights movements and God knows what all, the directors cut it from the budget. They did it against my advice, but I don't recall making too much of an issue out of it. The system, again.

Then, just as the fund drive was ready to begin, I had a visit from the leader of the Negro division of the Community Chest. This was another tradition, blacks and whites raising money separately, and the white community was happy if the Negro community added something like $40,000 to a total goal of $1,250,000. I had asked L. D. Milton, president of a Negro bank called Citizens Trust Company, to head the Negro drive that year, and he had accepted, and I had assumed I wouldn't hear from the Negro division until the fund drive was over. But here he was in my office—a proud black man, obviously better educated and more experienced than I, who would defer to no one and was the leader of his community that I would like to have been of mine—and he had a request. To his knowledge, he said, no member of the white leadership of the Community Chest had ever attended the opening fundraising dinner of the Negro division. Would I and R. G.

Taber, president of the Community Chest, consider going?

It is hard to believe now that such a simple request could cause a crisis, but it did. I was in a terrible quandary. I was a young man anxious to be successful in business and active in civic affairs—I suppose in the back of my mind I was already thinking about running for governor of Georgia someday—but I simply wasn't prepared to be asked to attend an all-Negro dinner. As I wanted guidance, I went to see Clark Howell and George Biggers, editors of the *Atlanta Constitution* and the *Atlanta Journal*, respectively. Neither was able to help me much, a situation like this being as new to them as it was to me. Finally I went to my father, who was seventy-one and turning the business over to me about this time.

In the context of that time, I would call my father a liberal. He used the term "nigger" without blinking, which was conventional then, but he didn't say it with malice. Thirty years earlier, during World War I, he had served a two-year term with honor in the Georgia legislature—his only actual political experience, although there were always rumors that he was going to run for governor or some other office—and when Franklin Roosevelt came along he was a big supporter of his social-welfare programs. Daddy's liberalism on the race issue was prompted by a businessman's pragmatism, certainly, but I think he did have a sense of guilt about the wrongs done the Negro and didn't know exactly what to do about it at his age.

"Ivan, let me have a very honest discussion with you," he said in his office the day I went to him. "My generation has completely failed in every way to enlighten or solve the major issue which our section of the country has: the racial issue. We haven't confronted ourselves with it. There is great prejudice, great trial and tribulation over the whole thing. We've kept the nigger not in a second-class but in a third- or fourth-class position, and as a result we've impoverished him and we've impoverished this section of the country. And the Southeast will never amount to anything until it brings its level of citizenship up. The very idea: here we are advocating human decency and freedom all over the world, and we find ourselves with dirty skirts at home. It's time for some major changes. Your generation is going to be confronted with it, and it will be the greatest agony that any generation ever went through."

After a minute or two I said, "What about the dinner?"

"That banker, Milton?"

"Yes, sir."

"Go."

I swallowed hard. "Daddy, I'll do what you say."

"Then I say you should go." There was a faint smile on his lips, and I asked him what was so funny. "Well, I'm sending you," he said, "but I wouldn't have the courage to do it myself."

The dinner was held at the Savoy Hotel, a dingy place in the heart of the Negro business district bordering downtown Atlanta. It was a balmy day in early fall, and when Taber and I arrived around seven o'clock there was a crowd of nearly five hundred Negroes already there, most of them dressed in their Sunday best and chattering away in the sweltering upstairs ballroom. This was the first time either of us had moved among so many black people, and although we were treated with considerable deference and courtesy it was a nervous situation for everybody. Taber and I, the only white people at the meeting, sat between Milton and another leader of the Negro community while the meal was served.

Afterwards it came time for the usual Community Chest report meeting. I had become accustomed to civic-club luncheons and other gatherings of white businessmen, which are generally bland and brisk and end right on time.

But it seemed that this was as much a social affair as it was a Community Chest report meeting, with much applause and cheering when a team captain would announce even the smallest pledge, and it looked like we were going to be there until midnight. The reports droned on, with team captains being introduced and roundly applauded and then giving their rambling introductory remarks and finally their skimpy reports. It became obvious quite early that the cheerleader of the group was a huge woman of perhaps three hundred pounds who sat in the front row in a tight blue knit dress covered with red paper feathers (this happened to be the Community Chest "Red Feather Drive"), and heaved up out of her chair and yelled "Hallelujah" at almost anything.

". . . the sum of forty-three dollars," a captain would say.

"Hallelujah Ay-*men*," the woman in the red-feathered dress would shout, touching off a spontaneous celebration.

I didn't see anything particularly wrong with it, although it was a scene I was unaccustomed to. I was thinking to myself that this must be what it is like in all of those decrepit African Methodist Episcopal churches out in the great sprawling rural South on hot summer Sunday mornings. But Taber, with a frown on his face, leaned over and whispered, "You're going to have to be careful about how you handle that situation."

Once all of the laborious reports had been presented, I gave the customary short pep talk and the meeting ended, except for the picture-taking and the handshaking. In those days, of course, it was quite a novelty for a Negro to shake hands with a white man. So everybody in the hall patiently waited, as though it were a formal receiving line, to shake hands with the two white Community Chest leaders who had come to their dinner. Taber and I were standing at the head table like that, having our hands shaken by an interminable procession of black hands, when all of a sudden there was a commotion in the crowd, and Taber excitedly leaned over to me again and said, "Watch out, she's coming!" I was shaking somebody's hand when suddenly the woman in the red feathers swept behind me and wrapped her bulging black arms around my neck. I didn't know who she was, or what she was doing, or what was going to happen next. Everybody in the room stopped moving. You could hear a pin drop. "Lord, God, chillun," the woman shouted, "this is *my baby*. I was his Mammy's nurse the night he was brung into this world!"

I don't know why Bertha Lewis and I didn't sit down and have a long talk once the crowd had finished cheering her and left the ballroom of the Savoy Hotel. There really wasn't much for us to talk about, I suppose. I never saw her or heard from her again. The experience that night stayed with me for quite a while, though, and I remember that a few days later I sat down and wrote out a check for $500, from the Ivan Allen Company to Mrs. Grace Hamilton, for national Urban League dues.

# Part One

# Enter, the Sixties

And they're trying to rebuild. Now, Miss Scarlett, don't say they are silly. You know Atlanta folks as well as I do. They are plumb set on that town, most as bad as Charlestonians are about Charleston, and it'll take more than Yankees and a burning to keep them away. Atlanta folks are . . . as stubborn as mules about Atlanta . . .

—Margaret Mitchell,
*Gone With the Wind*

Because they are manufacturing centers or because they are not thought of as being especially pretty, some American cities—Chicago, Pittsburgh and Detroit being good examples—are thought of in masculine terms and are referred to as "he." But when a city has a special charm or deals in lighter commerce—like Boston with its history and New Orleans with its French Quarter and San Francisco with its cable cars—it is regarded as feminine, as a lady. Atlanta, in spite of its birth in 1837 as a rowdy railroad town at the end of the line running south out of Chattanooga ("It was a small town with more saloons than churches . . . rough and noisy," says historian Franklin Garrett), has always seemed to her more poetic citizens and admirers the epitome of Southern womanhood: at once high-spirited and demure, frisky and languorous; cloaked in the romantic misconceptions of *Gone With the Wind* and the Old South. When General William Tecumseh Sherman burned Atlanta during the Civil War, leaving only four hundred of the city's 3,800 homes standing, it was considered by the South as a clear case of rape—a heathen Yankee had come in and violated one of our lovely daughters—and it took the better part of a century for Atlantans to forget. In the meantime, however, they also began to rebuild and to grow (the population doubled, to 22,000, between 1860 and 1870), and from this came the symbol that still stands for Atlanta today: the phoenix, the mythical Egyptian bird that arose from the ashes. By 1900 the population was pushing 100,-000, the people were talking about being at the crossroads of the Southeast—straight lines drawn from New York City to New Orleans and from Chicago to Miami will cross just north of the city—and for the first time Atlanta was being called the "New York of the South." She had very nearly been burned off the face of the map, but she had come back with a vengeance. Like the phoenix, she had arisen from the ashes.

By the middle of the twentieth century, Atlanta was truly the crossroads of the Southeast. Sitting on the southern edge of the Appalachian Mountains, the highest major city east of Denver, she benefited from geography: no extremes in weather, within reach of seacoasts and mountains alike, centrally located to become a major transportation hub. Population in the five-county metropolitan area pushed onward toward one million because in Atlanta there were a pleasant climate, jobs, entertainment, and housing. With the farms and the small rural towns dying all over the South, the young people began to flock to Atlanta and bring with them a fresh vibrancy of spirit. Birmingham and too many other Southern cities had long ago staked their futures on one major industry, but Atlanta had diversified partly by accident and partly by choice. Retail sales in Atlanta increased nearly six times between 1939 and 1958. By 1958, Atlanta had 12.8 per cent of the South's total wholesale sales and was about to take the lead in Southern factory production away from Birmingham. A sprawling network of interstate highways was on the drawing boards, and Atlanta's airport—it had been the second one built in the South—was ranked tenth in the nation in number of passengers. The city was well known as headquarters for large companies like Coca-Cola and Scripto, but Atlanta was now beginning to attract regional offices of national and international firms. And, not least, if there was an oasis for liberals in the South, it was Atlanta. Through the leadership of the *Atlanta Constitution*'s Ralph McGill and Mayor William B. Hartsfield—the latter, extremely progressive in his day, toward the end of a long reign at City Hall had coined the phrase, "The City Too Busy to Hate"—it seemed entirely possible that Atlanta would do a better job in the civil-rights struggle that was beginning to evolve than, say, Little Rock had done. On the eve of the sixties, Atlanta had become the capital city of the Southeastern United States. As economic consultant Philip Hammer wrote, Atlanta might be coming along just in time to do right what some other cities had done wrong: "Unlike the cities that reached the half-million and then the million mark 30 or 40 years ago, Atlanta is getting its size at a time of great mobility . . . Atlanta has the makings of a new kind of physical city. There is not much precedent for it."

But if you looked below the surface, you could see that Atlanta was starting to tread water. Only one major office building—the 22-story Fulton National Bank Building, tallest in town—had gone up in the previous thirty years. Since 1954 Georgia had slid from first to fifth place in the South in industrial development, something certain to have an adverse effect on the state's central distribution center. The city's growth rate had dropped behind other competitive cities, and it was being predicted that by the end of the sixties Atlanta would be lucky to rank as the Southeast's third largest city, behind Miami and Tampa-St. Petersburg. The city was suddenly failing to supply enough jobs to keep up with its population growth (indeed, in 1960, needing to gain a minimum of 10,000 new jobs each year, Atlanta *lost* 1,900 industrial jobs). Very little was being done in the way of promotion to attract new industry, and before industries were going to come Atlanta needed more supporting arms such as facilities for building and repairing machinery. We could talk all we wanted to about being progressive, but we were still being pulled down by a moldy state legislature and suspender-snapping politicians who continued to be elected through an unfair county-unit voting system whereby a tiny county in southeast Georgia could have almost as much to say about Atlanta's welfare —its share of state funds—as Atlanta itself. We could talk all we wanted to about being a "City Too Busy to Hate," but Atlanta was still detested and held back by one of the most racially spiteful states in America. We could talk all we wanted to about the benevolent leadership of our business community, but at this point there was a changing of the guard: the longtime old leaders were passing the mantle on to a whole new generation, and the leadership was not yet mature or solidified. So here we were, going into what would prove to be the most dynamic decade in the history of American cities, and instead of raising our sights and working toward becoming a *national* city we found that we were suddenly running in place and holding on as the leader of our region.

Like most of the younger business leaders who were emerging in Atlanta at that time, I had never once thought of living anywhere else. My family was of moderate circumstances during the years I was growing up, although my father was beginning to make a name for himself as a civic leader and his business was growing steadily each year. Like most kids in America during those days, I was motivated by the desire to have a business of my own and make a little money for myself. We lived on West Peachtree Street, about four miles from the middle of downtown Atlanta (which seemed like a long way out then), and I had a soft-drink stand on the sidewalk in front of our house. Whenever there was a major building project going on in the neighborhood during the summer months, I would carry the drinks over to the project and sell them to the workers for a nickel each, making about forty cents a case and accumulating a few dollars in the summer. I later enlarged that business by buying loaves of bread and potted ham, having my mother and our Negro cook make sandwiches for me, and then selling them for a nickel apiece at the streetcar turnaround on 17th and Peachtree.

I wasn't quite so enterprising in school. I always attended the Atlanta public schools—going to the Tenth Street and Spring Street elementary schools, and then to O'Keefe Junior High—and by the time I reached Boys' High School I had become a pretty sorry student. Our family had become a two-car family, and I got to drive a little four-cylinder Chevrolet coupe back and forth to school. I didn't pay much attention to my studies. I was more interested in having a good time, and like some kids get at one time or another I suppose I had the rather foolish idea that the world owed me a living. My record at Boys' High the first two years was so bad that I doubt if they would have let me stay in school if my father hadn't been such a prominent citizen. Once I simply signed my name to a blank sheet of paper and turned it in during a final examination in a biology class—the minute I looked at the questions on the exam I knew it was hopeless to try and answer them—and when the grades came back I had been given fifteen out of a possible hundred points. Still playing the smart-aleck, I made the mistake of asking the teacher in a very formal way why he had given me fifteen points for merely signing my name. "I thought it was worth at least *that* much," he told me, "because you not only *signed* it but you also spelled your name correctly." About my senior year, my attitudes began to change, and under somewhat desperate support and encouragement from my family— I was an only child—I began to study very hard and in the last quarter at Boys' High I made the honor roll.

The college I chose to go to just as the Depression was setting in was Georgia Tech, right there in Atlanta, and it was then that I developed a desire to be in the center of things. I enrolled in the School of Commerce, and the first year there I was one of only five students in the student body of about two thousand to make straight A's. I don't know exactly what had turned me around from being such a sloppy high-school student, but in those four years at Tech I was into almost everything and wound up graduating *cum laude* with one of the top two or three records in my class. I was president of the student body, vice-president of the Inter-Fraternity Council, cadet colonel of the Reserve Officers' Training Corps, president of ODK, vice-president of ANAK, and a member of the Dean's List. I tried to play football and baseball, and made the freshman basketball team. I knew the president, Dr. Marion Luther Britton, extremely well, and at one point led a student protest against Governor Eugene Talmadge when the Board of Regents abolished the School of Commerce at Tech and moved it to the University of Georgia for political reasons. In the summers I was able to go to a great boys' camp called Camp Greenbriar in Alderson, West Virginia, and one year, for serving as postmaster and stringing tennis rackets and counseling younger campers, I was paid $500, which I invested in Coca-Cola stock—my first investment and probably the greatest I ever made. Before I was graduated from Tech I even had the opportunities to pass the ROTC regiment in review for President Roosevelt and to hear Winston Churchill (not very well known then, of course) speak to the student body. Those were fine, exuberant years in school then, quite different from what it is like on a college campus today. But our exuberance was tempered by what was happening in the real world. We had entered Tech at a high point in the economic life of America, had been studying economics when the stock market crashed in 1929, and when we were preparing to go out on our own and make our way the country was in the depths of the Depression.

When I finished Tech, I was fortunate enough to receive many good job offers owing to my college record—and this was when there weren't many job offers at all. But I naturally wanted to go into the family business, which consisted of only the one Atlanta store then and in 1933 grossed $196,000 (today there are 15 stores throughout the Southeast, grossing nearly $16 million), and so I joined my father and his partner, Charles M. Marshall, at the Ivan Allen-Marshall Company for a salary of $100 a month. Three years later, when I had been boosted to $125 a month, I married Louise Richardson, of one of the most prominent families in Atlanta. I suspect that at one time Hugh Inman, Louise's maternal grandfather, was probably the wealthiest man in Atlanta—the foremost dealer in Atlanta real estate, a man who was willing to cancel a trade if the person he was dealing with raised any objection to it within a reasonable period of time. Louise's family had a great deal of property on Northside Drive, which is today no more than a twenty-minute drive from downtown, and so she and I as young marrieds moved into a small home out there and set up housekeeping. We had a fairly comfortable life, in spite of the $125-a-month income I was earning. We would take three or four big meals a week with relatives, and we had an excellent Negro maid named Viola Welch whom we paid six dollars a week (she was raised to seven dollars a week when the first child came) to cook meals and keep the house clean. I was working at my father's company, getting in a lot of golf at the country club near Mr. Marshall's home, beginning to participate in civic affairs such as Boy Scout and Community Chest work, and starting a family when Pearl Harbor was struck, and I was called into the army as a reserve officer. I spent the entire war in Atlanta with the Quartermaster Corps and the Selective Service system, something I thought at first was a lucky break but which turned out to be dull and personally embarrassing.

My first experience with politics (outside of serving once as a $2-a-day page in the Georgia legislature when my father was a legislator) had come in 1936 when Ed Rivers was elected governor of the state. My father, as a vigorous and outspoken Democrat and Roosevelt supporter, helped out on some of FDR's statewide fund-raising campaigns, and I fell in line with his thinking about the need for the type of social reforms that Roosevelt was carrying out. Daddy and I had to defend Roosevelt in the business community, which was our community, because FDR wasn't very popular there after his first term. Once Louise and I went to one of the fancy-dress balls at the Piedmont Driving Club as the "Landon Twins" (Alf Landon had carried only two states against Roosevelt), and few of our friends thought much of our brand of humor. Anyway, when Ed Rivers came along as governor of Georgia we jumped on his bandwagon because he seemed to have the same progressive

ideas as Franklin Roosevelt. I actively campaigned for
Rivers and served in a number of state-government posi-
tions during his administration between 1936 and 1940. As
treasurer of the State Hospital Authority, a neophyte getting involved in a sticky and potentially damaging political
venture, I raised $2.5 million by passing the state's first
revenue certificate bond issue—matching that with the
Public Works Administration money to rebuild the white
section of the old state mental hospital at Milledgeville (the
total budget of the State of Georgia in those days was
something like $30 million compared with $500 million
today). Although the Rivers administration was tarnished
by his association with a number of people who didn't have
the best reputations, he incorporated into Georgia the most
progressive programs the state had ever had up until that
time. Maybe it was the last really constructive program the
state has benefited from, because there had not really been
a major creative idea in the Capitol since Rivers' creation
of the state highway patrol and his social security acts of
the late thirties. During my association with the Rivers administration I began to get hooked on the idea of public
service. I came back into contact with an old college friend
of mine, Ellis Arnall, who had gone to the University of
Georgia and had been a student leader there, as I had been
at Georgia Tech, and Ellis eventually became state attorney general under Rivers. The Rivers administration ended
just before the beginning of the war, when Eugene Talmadge was elected again (Georgia governors could not
succeed themselves then, as now), and because the social
reforms of the thirties were under attack, most of us had
to go back into hiding.

When the war ended, on the day after Japan sued for
peace, Arnall, who had just been elected governor, went to
Washington and asked the Secretary of Defense to release
me immediately. They hadn't learned how to get people

out of the army yet, and it was all very complicated. But Arnall managed to spring me, and I immediately became executive secretary to the very young and vigorous and progressive new governor of Georgia. For the next dozen years almost all of my thoughts and actions were on the state level. I spent a year as Arnall's executive secretary and was chief of staff for M. E. Thompson, who moved into the governor's chair for two years (I had been the largest contributor in his campaign for lieutenant governor) during Georgia's famous "three governors" dispute. I served as a member of the state Board of Education and the state Department of Veteran Services, and over about a ten-year period I led the state Chamber of Commerce in industrial development projects, speaking at one time or another in almost all of Georgia's 159 counties. I eventually reached a point where I thought I might be a candidate for governor myself, and in 1958 I began feeling out my possibilities, touring the state, making speeches, shaking hands, seeing where I might find support. But a simple fact of life in those days was that, because the rest of Georgia was so much more conservative than Atlanta and because there was a county-unit election system to give the rural counties more strength than the urban areas, no Atlantan stood a chance of being elected governor. (It is ironic that the first Atlanta man to make it in modern times was Lester Maddox, who was most un-Atlantan.) I found this out very quickly. My moderate statements on the school desegregation issue following the Supreme Court's 1954 decision, my connections with "them lyin' newspapers" in Atlanta (as they were traditionally called by politicians like Talmadge and Marvin Griffin), and the fact that I was a well-bred and successful businessman in Atlanta forced me to abandon any thoughts about pursuing the job of governor any further. I dropped out of the race before it had even begun in earnest, and I turned my interests toward the city of Atlanta.

At that time the older white leaders of the city—men like Robert W. Woodruff, developer of the Coca-Cola company and possessor of the largest personal fortune in the South— were in the process of gracefully turning over the leadership to a younger group, of which I was a part. The older group, which included my father, had guided Atlanta from behind the scenes for nearly four decades. Sometimes altruistic but most often pragmatic—with a businessman's view that what was good for Atlanta was good for them— they had brought Atlanta from an overgrown country town to a metropolis totaling nearly one million people. Woodruff embodied the best of this group: for more than two decades he had been an unofficial advisor to Mayor Hartsfield, and I think it is correct to say that not a single fundraising drive in Atlanta during that time had been successful without help (usually in the form of an anonymous gift) from the Woodruff interests. Woodruff was the symbol of the benevolent, civic-minded patriarch. The year I headed the Community Chest campaign we went over our goal by $38,000, and because Woodruff had anonymously donated $100,000 to make the drive a success I wrote him that he was entitled to a rebate of $19,000—but he wrote back and told me to hold the money over until the next year's drive because "a rebate would just mess up my bookkeeping."

Now, however, Woodruff was turning over the management of Coca-Cola—and the direction of Atlanta, since the two functions were to a degree synonymous—to younger men, and his peers were doing the same. They had done a wonderful job in their time, but times were changing and they were the first to realize they were not prepared for the challenges of the second half of the twentieth century. We successors to the throne were expected to function just as they had: to love Atlanta, to cherish her, to guide her, to make her a better place than she was when we "inherited" her. It was not unlike the situation we had faced when we

had taken over the family businesses from our fathers. Indeed, it was concurrent.

This transferral of power had begun taking place in the
early fifties, but reached fruition in 1958 and 1959. When I
looked around to see who was with me in this new group
of leaders, I found my lifelong friends. Almost all of us had
been born and raised within a mile or two of each other
in Atlanta. We had gone to the same schools, to the same
churches, to the same golf courses, to the same summer
camps. We had dated the same girls. We had played
within our group, married within our group, partied
within our group, and worked within our group. We were
children of the Depression who had come out of it with
an appreciation of hard work, and we had been fortunate
enough to have certain benefits passed on to us from our
fathers so that our devotion to hard work—once the low
spot of the Depression passed around 1933—made it possible for us to enjoy spiraling success in business for all of
our years. It was not a particularly colorful group—the
fetish of Citizens & Southern National Bank President
Mills B. Lane for collecting antique cars was about as wild
as we got—and there were few escapades, scandals, or di-
vorces within our group. We were white, Anglo-Saxon,
Protestant, Atlantan, business-oriented, nonpolitical, moderate, well-bred, well-educated, pragmatic, and dedicated
to the betterment of Atlanta as much as a Boy Scout troop
is dedicated to fresh milk and clean air. That sounds corny
to a lot of people, especially to those in other cities whose
"white-power structure," as we were later to be called in
a not-so-flattering way, tended to be divided and not so
interested in the progress of their city as they were in their
own personal progress—but it was true about the business
leadership, the new civic leadership, in Atlanta at that
time. We *were* different in Atlanta. We were the presidents
of the five major banks, the heads of the Atlanta-headquar-

tered industries like Coca-Cola, the presidents of the three big utilities, the heads of the three or four top retail establishments, the managers of the leading national-firm branches for the Southeast, the man in charge of the city transit system, the heads of the larger local businesses such as the Ivan Allen Company and the Haverty Furniture Company, and the leading realtors. When you talked about the "power structure" or the "establishment" in Atlanta, you were really talking about the leaders of the top fifty or so businesses in the city. We had, for a dozen or so years, warmed up to our task by working on projects like the Boy Scouts Council and the Community Chest fund drive and various other good works, and now our time had come to replace our elders at the helm of the city. Nearly ninety percent of us lived inside a half-mile radius of the intersection of Habersham and West Paces Ferry roads, no more than ten miles from downtown Atlanta, and we had shared the same problems, interests, and ambitions our entire lives. We were concerned with executive problems: managing a firm, handling personnel, financing large projects, and handling taxes. This gave us a further common large bond, and it should not be surprising that we also constituted a separate social set—common backgrounds, common spirit, common interests, common goals—that was destined to evolve eventually into the business-civic leadership of the city: the "power structure."

On Christmas Day of 1959 I was talking with Ed Smith, president of the First National Bank in Atlanta and a close friend of mine for many years, about the problems the city was going to be faced with in the coming years. We discussed the general malaise the city was in at the time: little major building going on, jobs not keeping up with population growth, stirrings in the Negro community over racial inequality, the coming fight over school desegregation, the need to rejuvenate the downtown area, and so forth. I was vice-president of the Atlanta Chamber of Commerce then, about to step up to the presidency, and I had been doodling with a program I wanted to use as a guideline for the city when I became president for the year 1961. Following our conversation, Ed asked me to come down sometime later and discuss the whole thing with Jim Robinson, chairman of the board of First National Bank. All during that year I polished the program: actually a White Paper that would set objectives for Atlanta during the sixties, and with help from some of the best thinkers in the city I presented what had become known as the Six-Point Program to the Chamber. I didn't realize at the time how carefully this program would guide the city through the decade, how foreign it was to the political interests of the city, or how it would happen that much of the program would be accomplished without the help of City Hall. The points in the program were broad and simple, and it seemed that most of them could be accomplished more or less as a by-product of the business and civic community—my group of friends and business peers—if they continued on their unselfish course of trying to make Atlanta a better place to live in.

This is how the Six-Point Program was summed up in one piece of literature later published by the Chamber of Commerce:

SCHOOLS: The Atlanta Chamber of Commerce must take a bold and firm stand on this issue. It must clearly set forth to the public at large and the business community in particular the full implications of the Little Rock, Norfolk, and New Orleans stories. It should officially endorse the majority report of the Sibley School Committee (favoring keeping public schools open) and actively work for the passage of the necessary legislation in the January session of the General Assembly. Atlanta's public schools must stay open, and the Chamber should provide its share of vigorous leadership in seeing that they do.

EXPRESSWAYS: The Atlanta Chamber of Commerce must use its every facility to press for a definite step-up in the tempo of local expressway construction. To this end it should lend its full and continuous support to local, state, and federal agencies in all possible ways. Although the Chamber takes pride in what has been completed, it must at the same time insist that progress has not been fast enough and that a substantial acceleration in the expressway program is absolutely essential to the health and well-being of the Atlanta community.

URBAN RENEWAL: The Atlanta Chamber of Commerce must vigorously support the city's urban renewal and housing efforts across the board. More specifically, it should: (a) urge and assist in a speedup of activity by the city and its agencies handling the current program; (b) encourage private capital to take advantage of the unprecedented development opportunities in urban renewal projects; (c) press for a further expansion of urban renewal (including an expanded program of finance) in the years immediately ahead; and, (d) work with all agencies concerned in locating new housing opportunities for the Negro population.

AUDITORIUM-COLISEUM, STADIUM: The Atlanta Chamber of Commerce should strongly support the construction of an auditorium-coliseum and a stadium. Finance and building plans should be readied, sites selected, and operating organizations set up as rapidly as possible. The public wants these facilities, and there is no time to lose.

RAPID TRANSIT: The Atlanta Chamber of Commerce should take the lead in pressing for a practical, large scale rapid-transit system for Atlanta. The scope and timing of the project calls for an immediate start at concrete planning and programing. The only alternative is even more expressways than now projected at five times the cost per mile and even further expansion of automobile traffic loads, with a breakdown in central traffic circulation by the end of the decade.

"FORWARD ATLANTA": The Atlanta Chamber of Commerce should establish and vigorously carry out a three-year "Forward Atlanta" program of education, advertising, and research to carry the Atlanta story over the nation. This program should be supported by a minimum budget of $500,000 per year, raised from the Atlanta business community. Only through such a campaign can Atlanta hope to stay on top in the years ahead.

When I was named by the Chamber of Commerce in December 1960 to serve as president for the following year, and the Six-Point Program was unanimously accepted, we had charted our course as only we, as old-fashioned civic-minded businessmen, knew how. The Six-Point Program was a broad plan of development that could fall on its face if the businessmen making up the "power structure" in Atlanta didn't fully believe in it and take the initiative as they had always done in seeing that it was carried out. I felt confident that they would. I might not have felt so confident if I had known in advance what was ahead for us in the sixties.

It started in the spring of 1960, before I had even been sworn in as president of the Chamber of Commerce, when a group of students from predominantly-black Atlanta University petitioned the Chamber to listen to their grievances over the tight segregation policies at Rich's, the largest department store in the Southeast, and other downtown stores and cafeterias. Most of the board members of the

Chamber didn't even want to give the students an audience, but Mills Lane of C&S Bank and I led the argument that we should at least listen to them. So Mills and I were given the ball and told to meet with the students ourselves, as representatives of the Chamber. The students told us about how they could go into Rich's and buy all they wanted, but could neither take a seat at the lunch counters nor even try on clothes. It was, frankly, the first time Mills and I had given any thought to most of these difficulties faced by the Negro. We listened to them and said we would take the matter up with the other members of the Chamber, but then we made no serious moves toward eliminating segregation.

I think what we were doing was closing our eyes and hoping the problem would go away. It was in the nature of our upbringing that we had seldom come into contact with the problems of the Negro in America, except to note that our maids had to come an awfully long way from wherever they lived to get to our homes every day so they could clean our rooms and wash our dishes and mind our children, and we really had little preparation for something like this. A part of the Southern Way of Life was that you didn't really *see* Negroes when they were in a store or walking the streets downtown. You didn't happen to think that maybe they had no restroom to use while shopping, or that they had to buy dresses or slacks without first being able to try them on for size, or that when they became hungry they had the choice of either waiting until they got back to their own neighborhood grill or else sidling up, hat in hand, to the back door of a white man's restaurant and ordering something to go. I was on the board of directors at Rich's then, and we began discussing the students' demands, going so far as to determine the exact volume of Negro business, which wasn't much in dollar value, and giving consideration to making Rich's an all-white store. That is how naïve we were on the race issue at that point, on the verge of the greatest civil-rights struggle in the history of the United States.

Then, in the fall of that year, the students got tired of our procrastinating and took matters into their own hands. This was the era of the sit-ins, which had begun in Greensboro, North Carolina, and quickly spread throughout the South in a massive attempt to desegregate department stores and lunch counters. The sit-in movement was highly successful, desegregating hundreds of stores and lunch counters, and in the process giving birth to the Student Nonviolent Coordinating Committee and the theme song, "We Shall Overcome"—and now it was coming to Atlanta for the first time. One day about 75 students, led by Dr. Martin Luther King, Jr., who had recently moved back to Atlanta to run the Southern Christian Leadership Conference after the successful bus boycott in Montgomery, marched over the Hunter Street viaduct from the Atlanta University complex and descended upon Rich's. Once inside, they occupied the seats at one of the lunch counters there. When refused service, they continued to sit. A large crowd of angry whites began to form. The students still refused to move. They began to sing "We Shall Overcome." Rich's officials, having never been faced with anything like this before, lost their patience and called the police and had all of the students arrested.

Martin Luther King, Jr., came out on bail almost immediately, but became a national hero when he was promptly slapped with a six-month prison term for "breaking probation" by a judge in DeKalb County (Dr. King had been stopped earlier that year for driving with an Alabama license, and was fined and put on probation). We thought the students would grovel around and try to get the bail money up so they could get out of jail (in all, 180 were arrested), but we began to worry when a week passed and nothing happened. When Thanksgiving came they were still in jail. When Christmas came they were still in jail.

By the first of January 1961 the issue of the jailed students was beginning to boil over. The students were determined to stay in jail, sing freedom songs, and draw attention to the situation any other way they could until something was done about desegregation downtown. Atlanta was being criticized all over the nation for the crude way in which the situation had been handled. Branch offices were being pressured by their national headquarters because of the nationwide criticism and the decline in business. And most politicians were evading the issue because it was an election year. Mayor Hartsfield, being in the last year of a 23-year stay in office, had evidently decided not to get involved; he considered it a business issue rather than a matter for City Hall. In short, the issue was getting under everybody's skin.

Early in the year, a longtime Negro leader, Judge A. T. Walden, went by to see Rich's attorney, Robert Troutman, Sr., and then the two of them came over to the Ivan Allen Company to see me. They outlined the problem for me, as president of the Chamber, and for several days the three of us met and discussed the situation. (On one of these occasions, Judge Walden asked if he could use the restroom. This was the first time I came head-on with the problem of segregated restrooms. If I took him into any of the employee restrooms there, all hell would have broken loose in the company. I certainly couldn't ask him to go down and use the restrooms that were for Negroes only, because they weren't very well kept. I compromised by taking him into the private restroom that my father and I used, giving in on a personal basis.)

It was finally decided that the thing to do would be to call a meeting of the owners and managers of the leading twenty-five or so department, variety, and chain stores in the city to see if an agreement could be reached. I got in touch with the new executive vice-president of the Chamber, Opie Shelton—an aggressive young man fresh in from Baton Rouge who had strong segregationist feelings, I suspect, but was being thrown into the breach of the civil-rights struggle like the rest of us—and a meeting was arranged.

Troutman and I met with the store owners and managers, explaining the situation and asking them if they wanted us to try to resolve the issue with the black community. The joint opinion of these businessmen was clear: they were in a hell of a pickle. They were being criticized from all directions, and they didn't care to go on much longer like that. *Yes*, they said, *go ahead and work something out. Get us off the hook, even if it means desegregating the stores.* They were more liberal than the balance of the South, but the main thing guiding them was business pragmatism: *what's good for Atlanta is good for us; what's bad for Atlanta is bad for us.* Some of the old school, like Frank Neely, chairman of the board of Rich's, may have had some doubts. But when it came time to make a decision they never quavered. Without a dissenting vote, the twenty-five businessmen told Troutman and me to work out a settlement with the Negro community and be quick about it.

We then embarked on negotiations with the top two dozen Negro leaders in the city, Troutman turning over the representation of the white community to Shelton and me since he was first of all a lawyer representing Rich's. It was merely a matter of sitting down and talking it out, but that turned out to be not so simple, primarily because the black leaders were naturally suspicious of anything the white business community was willing to offer. They wanted to know in detail what we meant. Did we mean the Negro could try on clothes in a store? Try on shoes? Go into a beauty salon? Use the restrooms and water fountains? Not have COLORED stamped on the bills and advertising that came in the mail? Have a sandwich at the lunch counter? Use the same elevators and stand in the same lines as white customers? Negotiations seemed to be limitless, compounded by the fact that the Negro representatives still had the habit of allowing each other to make rambling speeches rather than getting to the heart of the matter and coming up with a businesslike decision. These meetings took place almost every afternoon for some five weeks in conference rooms at the exclusive Commerce Club (unknown to the members of the Commerce Club, who had strict rules against Negroes using the facilities there), and it took all of the patience Opie Shelton and I, accustomed to fast-moving meetings, could muster.

Finally, after all of this, we began to arrive at a very simple agreement. Within thirty days after the court-ordered desegregation of Atlanta public schools in the fall, we would guarantee the full desegregation of downtown stores and lunch counters. Meanwhile, all picketing and boycotting would cease, and the students would be released from jail with all charges against them being dropped. We asked Dr. Rufus Clement, president of Atlanta University, to write out the agreement and present it to his committee for approval. The black leaders endorsed the contract, which is what it amounted to, and when I called the white businessmen together they quickly accepted it. Then we asked Judge Walden to take the agreement to the Atlanta newspapers and make the announcement, and we sat back and waited for panic to set in.

And there *was* panic. A great number of people canceled their account with Rich's and some of the other stores which had joined in the agreement. There was quite a crowd that said the white community had been sold out.

There were a lot of people who said they were going to move out of Atlanta. Lester Maddox—operator of the Pickrick Restaurant, a fried-chicken emporium, who was just beginning to make national headlines as a segregationist—resigned from the Chamber of Commerce for the umpteenth time. But then the fires began to burn out. We had deliberately written a delay clause into the contract to allow time for fever to subside in the white community and to have the court-ordered school desegregation sustaining our position. The students were released from jail, the national spotlight swung away from Atlanta, home offices took the heat off their chain-store managers, and picketing ended. It looked like we had made it over the hump simply by sitting down and bringing the black and white community leaders together on a businesslike basis.

Soon after the agreement was announced, however, we were surprised and disheartened to see resentment building up in the black community over the delay clause. Suddenly many of the younger black leaders, some of whom had been jailed during the sit-ins at Rich's, were threatening more demonstrations if there weren't immediate desegregation. The white community had reluctantly accepted the agreement as inevitable, but there was great turmoil in the black community. Almost every day, it seemed, there was another mass meeting being called at a Negro church somewhere to discuss what the black people of Atlanta should do: wait the few extra months, or demand their rights *now?* We were bailed out of this crisis by Dr. Martin Luther King, Jr., who had been released from Reidsville State Prison at the request of John and Robert Kennedy. This was the first time I ever actually saw Dr. King in action, and it was to lead to a long and close friendship between us.

One of those meetings was held one night at the Wheat

Street Baptist Church, one of the largest Negro churches in the South. Its pastor was the Reverend William Holmes Borders, who had forced the desegregation of public transportation in Atlanta by being the first Negro to ride up front in a city bus. As president of the Chamber and someone who had been working on the problem all along, I was asked by the Reverend Mr. Borders to attend the meeting. A huge, impassioned crowd jammed the big church and the meeting got completely out of hand very quickly. The young ones wanted to go into the streets. They were joined by some of the older and more respected leaders, including a well-known dentist who claimed they had been sold out. It was frustrating to those of us who had worked so hard and so long to come up with a workable agreement that would finally solve Atlanta's stickiest issue. Neither Mr. Borders nor Dr. King, Sr., could control the crowd. It looked like the whole thing was going to blow up in our faces, just when we thought we had everything worked out.

Then, at the high point of the explosion, in walked Martin Luther King, Jr. I had read about him and heard about him from his father, but I had not been able to imagine just how much charisma he actually had. No one had to introduce him, of course, because he had already become the champion of the civil-rights cause. The minute he entered the church and began walking firmly and confidently toward the pulpit the shouting stopped. All eyes were on him. He took to the pulpit and stood before the crowd for a full minute, searching every face in the audience. It became deathly quiet.

Finally he said, "I'm surprised at you. The most able leadership you could have to represent you has made a contract with the white man, the first written contract we've ever had with him. And now I find people here who are not willing to wait another four or five months, after waiting one hundred years and having nothing to show until now." He said he would hold every Negro citizen of Atlanta personally responsible to him for the fulfillment of the contract. "If this contract is broken, it will be a disaster and a disgrace. If anyone breaks this contract, let it be the white man." And he left, as quickly and mysteriously as he had come. I had heard him called "Little Jesus" in the black community. Now I understood why.

# Allen for Mayor

[Allen] seems more intent on living up to his
name than on living on it. If he desired approbation he would shrink into his set and settle
for tea, tennis and tired blood. He has repeatedly chosen to go into combat . . .

—Editor Eugene Patterson's column
in the *Atlanta Constitution*, March 1961

As we worked out the details of the contract between the
black community and the downtown stores, some of the
Negro leaders started mentioning the mayor's race to me.
They had supported Mayor Hartsfield for all of these years,
and now that he appeared to be stepping down they were
forced to look around and choose his successor—above all,
someone who was most likely to carry on the race issue with
moderation, as Hartsfield had done for more than two decades. It was inevitable, I suppose, that they would turn to
me. For several weeks we had been closely collaborating,

trying to work something out on the desegregation of the stores and lunch counters, and it was the first time in Atlanta history that a leader of the white business community had sat down with the leaders of the black community and fashioned a joint contract of this nature. So we had gotten to know each other, and soon Walden and King, Sr., and Borders were asking me to run for mayor and telling me they would throw the support of the entire black community behind me.

The idea of running intrigued me, but at first I didn't take it very seriously. After my abortive attempt at running for governor in 1958 I had given up any thoughts about being actively engaged in politics. The Ivan Allen Company needed me, my family needed me, and the Chamber of Commerce needed me. I felt I could do just as much good for the city if I continued to work for it simply as a concerned businessman, rather than as mayor. But as spring of 1961 came there was more and more talk about me as a possible candidate, from the black *and* white leadership. I'd had a world of favorable publicity over the years, particularly during the negotiations with the black community over desegregation. There was a lot of talk within the Chamber about my Six-Point Program, and about how the desegregation issue had been worked out so smoothly. One night at a dinner in honor of a delegation which had come from the West Coast on a Delta Air Lines inaugural flight, after I made the Chamber of Commerce pitch, John White —who had been active in city politics for 35 years and was the oldest alderman—said aloud to the visiting politicians at his table, "You just heard the next mayor of Atlanta, and I'm going along with him." I heard the rumbling, naturally, but didn't seriously contemplate running for office until a flattering editorial appeared in *Constitution* Editor Eugene Patterson's column one morning in early spring:

Ivan Allen, Jr., is a fairly representative figure of the concerned Southerner. Fairly young, solid financially, born well and bred to pride in the South. Many who are like him recline on the soft fronds of comfort and observe the passing world. But Ivan Jr. concerns himself with the scenes that pass, as his father did, and this kind of latter-generation involvement in life reflects credit on the ancestry as well as the man.

To call this earnest businessman ambitious, in the uncomplimentary sense, is inaccurate. He seems more intent on living up to his name than on living on it. If he desired approbation he would shrink into his set and settle for tea, tennis and tired blood. He has repeatedly chosen to go into combat.

Three years ago he even announced for governor. After a round of civic club speeches and general soundings he swallowed his pride and withdrew with the frankest excuse we've heard lately; he said he had discovered he couldn't win.

He did not turn in his sword and relax with a martini, however. He learned and laid aside his lesson in state politics without rancor, and plowed his intense blend of idealism and pragmatism back into the earth of Atlanta. He is the kind of practical businessman who believes in "no nonsense" and "sound judgment." But he has not drifted into the nonsensical slough of the narrow mind which believes its own findings, arrived at without touch with the straining masses, has hemmed up the final word and been knighted for it. He is not content with what he can do for himself; he is concerned with what he can do for people. And that is a pretty noble thing.

So it is not at all surprising to find Ivan Allen, Jr., had a hand in working out the enormously important solution to the sit-in problem in Atlanta—not on the pattern of any other town, but on a new pattern pioneered in this city.

Robert Troutman, Sr., erect and honorable believer in both white pride and progress, and A. T. Walden, a Buddha-like advocate of so much Negro pride and wisdom, turned to the president of the Atlanta Chamber of Commerce seeking the cohesion necessary to make an agreement fair to all, and to make it stick.

The Chamber president was Mr. Allen. He did not duck behind his board or his bylaws. He waded into the deepest emotional impasse of this decade. He did not follow any mimeographed lobbyist sheet for dealing with "antibusiness elements," but instead followed the instincts of a sound and altruistic man who weighs the alternatives and chooses. Short months ago, after he had urged the Chamber to support open schools, he had declined pressures to set up biracial negotiations on sit-ins.

He did not believe it was right or possible then to do so. But when growth of mutual respect made it so, Ivan Allen, Jr., supported by the Chamber, was not so hamstrung by his city's past that he refused to give his hand to its future. With Mr. Troutman and Mr. Walden, and all the people they spoke for, he brought Atlanta to a better morning this morning, and this place is lucky to have a fellow like that.

Then one morning in April Mills Lane walked into my office and, in his casual way, grinned and threw a double-faced mailer on my desk. It was what the trade calls a "twelve-cent mailer." You send it out intact and the reply comes back on the one half, which is perforated and can be torn off. I picked it up and saw that it had one simple question printed on the side to be returned: "Do you think Ivan Allen, Jr., would be a good candidate for mayor of Atlanta?" First of all, I was shocked that Mills had gone this far in his thinking about me as a candidate without even talking to me about it. Secondly, I didn't think it would prove anything. It amounted to a popularity contest, more than anything else. You don't get many negative replies on these things, because it isn't worth the trouble to be negative.

"Have you already printed these things?" I said.

"Sure have," Mills told me.

"When did you think about it?"

"About four o'clock this morning."

"When did you print them?"

"About eight o'clock this morning."

"When will you mail them out?"

"They've already gone out."

I was stunned. My doubts about the value of the mailers to the contrary notwithstanding, it did seem like a generous thing for him to do. I figured he had sent out about a thousand of them, which would cost $120. But Mills said he had mailed out approximately 88,000 of them, and that would mean nearly $11,000 at twelve cents each. As a stockholder in his bank I said, "Mills, you can't spend the C&S Bank's money for something like this."

"I didn't," he said. "I paid for it myself."

It didn't take the press long to find the poll in the mail, of course. They were beating on Mills' door the next few days as the postcard replies began to come back in. To my surprise, there was a flood of returns that reached nearly ten thousand—an excellent response—and they were almost 100 per cent favorable. Of course, they hadn't been asked and hadn't said whether they would actually go out and *vote* for me. At any rate, Mills finally began to release the results of the poll and soon I was being mentioned as a candidate almost every day in the papers. The green light had been switched on with a batch of twelve-cent postcards asking one simple question.

As I began to think seriously about running I studied my chances, and everything seemed promising. The experience with the black leaders had apparently gained their respect for me, and I felt I could count on their support. Although there was as yet no united front in the so-called "white power structure," these were my close personal friends— my generation—and I felt I would be able to depend on them. I had the friendship of the media, and could hope for their endorsement. I had a good family name, thanks to my father. I felt I knew how to campaign, after being close to state government and helping out in numerous political campaigns for a dozen years or so. And I felt I had a high recognition factor: the Ivan Allen Company did more local advertising than any other company of its size in Atlanta, and panel trucks with IVAN ALLEN on the side were always on the streets. This factor spoke eloquently when our salesmen conducted a random poll in the four quadrants of the city, and I received seventy-five per cent support.

One last question had to be answered before I could decide to run for mayor of Atlanta. I had to know if William B. Hartsfield really did intend to step down or if he was going to stay on at City Hall, in which case I would have stayed out of the race. I wanted Helen Bullard—a lady with a remarkable track record in Atlanta and Georgia political races—to be my campaign manager, and when I talked to her about it she said she would like to help me but she was committed to help Hartsfield and even *she* didn't know what he was going to do. As time was too short for me to wait for Hartsfield to say whether he intended to run again, I had to take the bull by the horns.

I made an appointment with him for two o'clock one afternoon, but he didn't walk into his office until 3:15. Then, for forty-five minutes, he paced the floor and talked about the hardships of being mayor: the stacks of papers that had to be signed and the unwillingness of the board of aldermen to cooperate with him. ("They're either out drinking martinis, or playing golf, or out of town.") For a total of two hours, then, I had been sitting around waiting to ask him one simple question.

When I finally got a chance I said, "Mr. Hartsfield, I wonder if you'd let me make a statement?"

"Go ahead," he said.

"I think you can be re-elected. I'll put ten thousand dollars in your campaign fund and take a leave of absence from my company so I can be your campaign manager. I can help you with the younger people, and you can be re-elected."

He said, "You wouldn't make an offer like that unless you wanted something, now, would you?"

"No, sir," I said. "If you're *not* going to run, I'd like for you to make an announcement so that the rest of us can get in the race."

He went over to the window and stood there for a few minutes, mumbling to himself as the afternoon light played over his tired hulking frame and accented the wrinkles on his hands and neck. When he turned around he sounded like a very old, very tired man. "I've had this job for twenty-three years," he said. "I'm seventy-two years old, and I've been married for forty-eight of 'em, and now I'm in love with a very wonderful young lady and I want to marry her. I can't get a divorce and be re-elected mayor. If you'll send Helen Bullard over here tomorrow, I'll make my announcement and get out of the race so you boys can go on about your business. I've been around long enough." He gave no evidence that he would support me—he never did take a stand in the race that was to come—but he had finally cleared the air. After more than twenty-three good years at the helm, he was making way for a new era at City Hall. I resigned as president of the Chamber of Commerce and announced my candidacy.

Now it was time to get into the sweaty business of campaigning, and I was already ahead of the four other candidates in several very important areas. Thanks to the support of Mills Lane and the rest of the business community, not to mention a good stockpile of my own money, I had more than enough funds to run a professional campaign. I also had a ready-made organization, some four hundred employees of the Ivan Allen Company who were always loyal and ready to help whether we needed a good crowd for a rally or help on a city-wide poll. And, too, I had the best brains in Atlanta at my disposal: Helen Bullard as campaign manager, most of the leaders of the black and white business communities as unofficial aides and advisors (Cecil Alexander, a personal friend and highly successful architect, took a leave of absence for six weeks to help run my campaign), and even some outside assistance (either Charles Smithgall or Sylvan Meyer of the newspaper up the road in Gainesville was at my side every day of the race, on the theory that what was good for Atlanta was good for northeast Georgia). Finally, and not to be overlooked, right off the bat I received the public endorsement of the five major bank presidents. I was, of course, the choice of the business community—the "silk-stocking" candidate.

One indication of the solidarity of the support I had in the business community and the way we were all united in interests and goals was to come early in the campaign. The sixth candidate was Howell Smith, a tax consultant, who was ordered out of the race when the check for his $2,500 entry fee bounced. Howell was an enthusiastic candidate who injected the sense of humor that any political race needs to keep it sane, and even after he was scratched he continued to attend the joint rallies and appear on the platform and make his speeches.

At one of those meetings, about two weeks after Howell had dropped out, he sidled up to me and said, "Allen, I'm going to support you." As I had already learned that you don't turn down anybody's support in a campaign, I thanked him.

"You know why I'm going to support you?" he said.

"No, I don't, Mr. Smith, but I appreciate it."

"Well, I'll tell you why," he said, launching into a long story. "When I found out that Mills Lane and the C&S

Bank were backing you, I figured I'd get me a bank to back me. So I called up Mr. Ed Smith over at First National and went over there and he said, 'I'd be delighted to support you, because I'm sure you'd make a good mayor. But Ivan and I are very close personal friends, and our wives were born and raised together and have traveled together all their lives, so we're just committed to support Ivan.' He was very gracious about it, and I wasn't too upset. I knew I had three more banks, anyway. Well, next I went to see Mr. George Craft at the Trust Company of Georgia, and he was nice to me, too, said he would even support me— except, he said, you two were raised together and your daddy is a director of the Trust Company of Georgia, and Mrs. Craft and your wife had traveled together all over the world, so he was going to have to support his friend Ivan Allen, Jr. Well, that shook me a little but I still had two banks left, so I went to see Mr. Gordon Jones at the Fulton Bank, and he told me you two were fraternity brothers, and his wife and Mrs. Allen had just spent the summer in Europe together. That left me one more bank, the National Bank of Georgia, and I never saw anybody so gracious in my life as Mr. Joe Birnie. He said he thought I'd make a fine candidate, just like everybody else had said. But then I got the same thing. 'Ivan Allen and I are good friends,' he said, 'and on top of that, my wife and his spent the spring traveling together in Europe, so I'm going to have to support Ivan.'"

By this time we were both laughing. "Tell me something," Howell said.

"What's that?"

"Are you running for mayor, or is Mrs. Allen running a *travel bureau?*"

There is no way to describe properly how deeply involved you can get in a political campaign—you, your family, your friends, your supporters, your campaign workers. It captivates everybody around you, and everything you do is overshadowed by the race at hand. We put together a large, well-oiled machine and developed what was regarded at that time as fairly sophisticated strategy: sending out a lengthy questionnaire to every registered voter in the city, asking for advice on the issues of the day, tabulating the results and releasing them to the press; and arranging for a series of polls in all fifty-nine precincts so we would know at all times how we stood. (John F. Kennedy had made good use of polls during his campaign for the presidency, and we took the cue from him.)

It seemed obvious that I should run on a promise of continued prosperity, emphasizing my background as a business leader and as former president of the Chamber of Commerce, talking about Atlanta's future role as a national city rather than merely a regional distribution center. This was my strong suit, the place where I had a clear edge over the other four candidates. None of them had the personal associations in the higher echelons of the city that I had. None of them had the experience of doing big business, of dealing in terms of millions of dollars. We were going to take a safe, solid middle-of-the-road position. We were going to keep accurate polls. We were going to spend money. We were going to speak positively about prosperity and growth, about the Six-Point Program, about the promise of the years ahead in Atlanta. We were going to play it straight and win on finesse and power.

I changed my mind before the first rally. It was going to be held at night in an elementary school, with all of the candidates on hand, and while I nervously ate an early dinner at home that night I started thinking about it a little deeper. Here I was with a typical Chamber of Commerce speech to give Atlanta voters, and yet I knew how shallow it was at a time like this. Little Rock had virtually died on the vine when it failed to face the school-integration issue realistically four years earlier. I could promise all I wanted to about Atlanta's bright, booming economic future, but none of it would come about if Atlanta failed to cope with the racial issue. That, I knew, was the *real* issue in this campaign: was Atlanta going to be another Little Rock, or was Atlanta going to set the pace for the New South? And I was quite aware that my most serious opposition would come from Lester Maddox, who had unsuccessfully run for mayor against Hartsfield in 1957. Maddox, a 10th-grade dropout who ran a blue-collar fried-chicken restaurant called the Pickrick, had sprung out of the lower- and middle-class white neighborhood suddenly when the Supreme Court handed down its decision on school desegregation. As polarization set in, his star rose higher. Undoubtedly he would scream "nigger-nigger-nigger" throughout the campaign. Almost every leading politician in the South was advocating massive segregation laws, threatening to close the schools if there was a single effort made to integrate them, accusing the Supreme Court of turning Communist, wallowing in the debate over segregation and integration of the races. Through my actions during the sit-ins and through some pragmatic public statements I had made in the late fifties about school desegregation ("To abandon public education is to secede from the economic life of our nation, and that we cannot afford," I said in late 1958), I had already gained a liberal reputation that had cost me a position on the state board of regents in 1960 when Governor Ernest Vandiver indicated he would appoint me if we could reach an "understanding about the racial problem," and I refused to say I would go along with closing public schools. It was time, I thought, for somebody to stand up for what's right; and it might as well be me, since I was already committed on desegregation. Without finishing dinner, I got up from the table and called Helen Bullard.

"I'm not going to make that speech," I told her.

"You're not—"

"I'm going to jump on Maddox."

"What?"

"Nobody's ever attacked him or his kind down here," I said. "I think it's time somebody told him we're not going to let him and his crowd destroy Atlanta. I want to jump on him hard, Helen, and tell him we're going to hold him responsible for his actions. What do you think?"

"Well, Ivan, I don't know."

"You're my campaign manager."

She deliberated a few seconds and then said, "If you feel that, and feel it very strongly, go ahead and do it."

I spoke out that night, at the leadoff rally in the campaign, and it completely stunned Maddox. He had always been good on his feet, always tough in an alley fight, but he was so taken aback by my attack that he didn't know what to say. "You represent a group which would bring another Little Rock to Atlanta," I said, looking directly at Maddox as I spoke. I don't have a copy of exactly what I said, and couldn't even remember much of it the next day, because I was speaking from the gut without notes. When it came time for Maddox to speak at the rally, he could only sputter: "The pinks, radicals, and Communists are trying to eradicate freedom while I am trying to protect your homes, your jobs and your churches . . . We are teaching love and racial pride . . ." And so forth. The debate was splashed all over the papers the next day, of course, and the initial reaction around town was, *Ivan really blew it last night, he committed suicide before the first rally was over.* My opponents naturally came out with statements saying I was already out of the running. I didn't know what the effect would be. As it turned out, I had drawn the battle line early between Maddox and me, and none of the other candidates was ever able to get into contention after that first rally.

If I learned anything in that campaign that would be of value to me in later years, it was how to deal with the Lester Maddoxes. Those people have never been able to understand happiness, regardless of their pretensions toward religious joy. I learned to smile or laugh at Maddox whenever he unloaded another of his endless ridiculous accusations, and it was like puncturing a balloon. You could do that, or you could try to stay a step ahead of him. At one rally Maddox charged that a number of the candidates had gone to a Negro meeting at Frazier's Café, in the Negro section, the night before. It was true. Everybody had gone except Lester Maddox. Well, I saw one of the other candidates wither under the accusation and slip out of the back of the hall rather than have to reply to Maddox's charge. I told the crowd that, yes, I was there and I saw nothing wrong with it, and when I got back to my headquarters I decided to go on the offensive again. I told Helen Bullard I wanted my schedule of appearances—*all* appearances—to run each week in every Atlanta newspaper, including the black *Atlanta Daily World.* There had always been a sort of gentleman's agreement in Atlanta that no publicity would be given a candidate's contacts with the Negro community. Once it was brought out into the open like that, there was no mystery to it and the sting was gone from Maddox's attack.

As the summer wore on, it was clearly a battle between the anti-integration of Lester Maddox and my stand for moderation and understanding. When I look back I am amazed at how little we actually knew about the racial issue then. The only major racial issue involved in that campaign was whether you wanted to have open schools or were willing to close public schools in order to avoid integration. We were so naïve. There had been no civil-rights bill proposed. There were no authorities on the problem, no learned solutions, few people speaking out about it in public. It simply boiled down, at that point in history, to whether you were for integration or segregation. And although I had been the proponent of the desegregation of Atlanta's downtown stores and lunch counters and had worked out the agreement with the black community, something that had not yet been put into effect, I was caught in the crossfire. The black voters weren't supporting me because the desegregation hadn't been accomplished, and my support in the white community was slipping because I had helped draw up the agreement.

The opposition against me from the racists in town got so rough that soon we began to receive anonymous threatening phone calls at home. All of the calls were based on the race issue, and as time went by they became more and more vicious. Louise and I weren't much concerned about the calls in the beginning, but then they started making threats about our children—"We're gonna sic a pack of mad dogs on your boys," and that sort of thing. Our two oldest boys were virile young men who could take care of themselves, but our youngest son was only nine years old. A couple of times he raced to answer the telephone first, as kids will do, and heard the threats himself. He was an intelligent boy, but he couldn't grasp the vileness of these things being said to him. So I called Herbert Jenkins, the chief of police, and explained the situation. Legally, it was impossible then for a candidate to have a police escort. So Chief Jenkins furnished me, at my expense, two detectives to work alternate nights from 4 P.M. to 8 A.M. the following morning—eating with us and then sleeping in the same room with Beaumont, our nine-year-old. Beaumont had a field day, of course, hearing honest-to-goodness cops-and-robbers stories from armed policemen; and one of the two detectives, George Royal, became such a member of the family that he became my trusted aide when I went into office.

As the race went down to the wire, our polls told us we were sliding. We still had the lead, but we were losing the conservative vote to Maddox and weren't picking up enough strength in the black community to offset it. We had opened up a campaign headquarters in the heart of the Negro business section and paid young black workers to make telephone solicitations in my behalf, but as we came to the last week of the campaign we knew we had to do something about the Negro vote. Muggsy Smith, a white insurance man, was hurting us there by pointing out that desegregation had not yet been accomplished and by pounding away at my position as the "white-power structure's man." During that last week of the race, on the eve of a large political rally at a Negro church, we got word that Smith's people were going to try to stampede the black vote by showing up with an impressive crowd of his own black supporters.

So we began to lay plans to offset what was obviously going to be the last-ditch stand of the Smith forces in the Negro community. What we would do was throw a free supper open to the public earlier in the evening, and then charter buses and carry *our* people down to the rally. We chose the Walahauga, a fairly modern hotel that had a large ballroom and was at that time *the* place for large Negro social gatherings. The builder and owner of the Walahauga was an influential Negro builder named Chief Aiken, who had once bought a collie puppy from us (when the puppy didn't turn out right we gave him another, which led to a long friendship between the Aikens and the Allens). As Chief Aiken was a supporter of mine, I went to him and began arranging for a huge dinner. There would be barrels of fried chicken, gallons of Coke, a minimum of speech-making, and a lot of music from Graham Jackson, a popular Negro entertainer. We posted notices about the supper in all of the large stores and manufacturing plants, reserved twenty buses from Atlanta Transit to carry the crowd to the rally after the Walahauga bash, and sat back to await the big night.

We had been planning on a crowd of about eight hundred people, but twice that number showed up and we had to put in a frantic order that night for twenty more buses. After the supper and the entertainment, we invited everybody there to get on a bus and go with us to the rally about eight or ten blocks away from the Walahauga. I went ahead in a car and when I got to the church where the rally was being held I found Muggsy Smith standing outside, looking smug, with about fifty supporters intent on putting on an impressive show of strength for him. Then, all of a sudden, these forty buses with ALLEN FOR MAYOR signs on them started rolling up to the church and spilling out their thousand or so well-fed and recently converted Allen supporters. I had to feel sorry for poor Muggsy. The color went out of his face when he realized what was happening. When he spoke at the rally he was all by himself, because his fifty-odd supporters had wilted at the sight of our thousand and slowly drifted away.

On the morning of the election Joe Heyman, vice-president of the Trust Company of Georgia, the man who had refined our polling techniques to the point that the poll was now totally reliable, told me how the vote would go. I would get 38 per cent of the vote, he said, and Maddox would be second with 21 per cent. This would mean a runoff between the two of us, since it took at least 50 per cent of the votes cast to win, and that was fine with me: in a head-to-head confrontation with Lester Maddox, I felt I could easily win by getting all of the black vote and perhaps half of the white.

There isn't a lot a candidate can do on election day but sweat. When Joe Heyman gave me the projected vote totals, based on our polls, I sat in my office and tried to think of what I could do with that information I had. Donald Hollowell came to mind. Don was a prominent Negro lawyer in town who had run Smith's campaign and managed, according to our poll, to obtain about 10,000 of the city's 35,000 Negro votes on his own popularity. Muggsy hadn't had to raise a finger for it. I had never understood why Don Hollowell and I weren't working together in the race, because we had been good friends (he had represented some of the students during the sit-ins) and had a mutual respect for each other. I thought I would give him a call and tell him what our poll said was going to happen that day. I would need him tomorrow.

When I called and told the girl who answered that Ivan Allen, Jr., was calling, I heard a gasp. Mr. Hollowell wasn't in, she said, but she would have him return the call. He called in a couple of minutes, somewhat shocked that I would be calling, and after we parried I said, "I'm calling to ask your support."

"Apparently, Mr. Allen, you don't realize I'm with Mr. Smith."

"But what about tomorrow?"

"What?"

"I'm going to be in the runoff, and I need your help."

"Well," he said, "I feel Mr. *Smith* is going to be in the runoff with Maddox, and that we're going to need *your* help."

I said, "That's not the case, Mr. Hollowell. I know what the vote is going to be. We've polled it." I gave him the breakdown and impressed him with the mechanics of our poll. I knew the wheels were spinning in his head. "Your candidate is going to finish fourth with 14 per cent of the vote. I'm asking if you'll support me in the runoff."

"Mr. Allen," he said, without hesitating, "If you're right, I'll be the first person in there tomorrow morning." And he was. The vote went exactly as our poll had projected, and we went into a runoff with Maddox with all the confidence in the world. There would be two additional weeks of campaigning before the runoff election would be held. We didn't have to worry about not getting the Negro vote any more, and we weren't concerned with a formidable opponent. We weren't even concerned about financing the extra two weeks of politicking, because on the morning after the primary my father came into my office—a gray-haired man whose generation had struggled for every dime and saved half of it—and he said, "How's your campaign?" We had spent about $175,000 to that point.

"We've managed to pay our bills so far," I said.

"Got any money left over?"

"No, sir."

"What's this other two weeks going to cost?"

"I don't know, Daddy. Whatever's necessary."

"Well," he said, "when you get through, send me a bill for half of it." And he turned and walked out. Maddox had been accusing us of spending a lot of money during the campaign, so we saw no reason why we shouldn't go ahead and do it if we were going to be accused of it. In the runoff I received 65 per cent of the vote, and in the Negro precincts I wiped him out: 21,611 votes to his 237.

Maddox wasn't through yet, of course, not by a long shot. There were his usual pronouncements about how I was the Communist candidate and was going to bring about "race-mixing" and other catastrophes, and then a ludicrous charge that I had "bought Negro votes"—the latter the result of a twenty-dollar handout I had given to an old black friend in need, Grant Carter.

I had known Grant Carter for as long as I could remember. When I was a child he was the livery man and chauffeur for the Edward Inmans, Louise's aunt and uncle, who lived in a beautiful estate on Peachtree Circle. My cousin lived across the street from them, and we spent so much time as small boys playing with young Edward Inman that we were more or less raised under the influence of Grant Carter, who looked after us and regaled us with stories as we gamboled around the barn, the lawn, and the carriage house. Later, when Mr. Inman died, Grant went to work for Robert Woodruff and became, in effect, a chauffeur for dignitaries of Coca-Cola—and that was in the days when chauffeuring was a high calling. Then Grant retired with a small pension and fell on hard times, and I could count on his coming by my office before Christmas and maybe in the summer, and in the spirit of Old South paternalism I would always slip him a five- or ten-dollar bill. From my office he would proceed to my father's, getting the same result, and he had a pretty good trade all over town among these people who had known him every bit as long as I had.

When I entered the mayoralty campaign, Grant was one of the first older Negro citizens to come and see me and pledge his support, saying he would do whatever he could to help me get elected. And he kept his word: he was always on the periphery at rallies, a highly respected man who had chauffeured the mighty and didn't let his friends in the black community forget it. Anyway, several days after I had won the election, Grant Carter called me up the day before I was leaving for Europe on an inspection tour of the Berlin Wall with other elected officials, and we chatted for a few minutes.

"Mr. Ivan," he said, "we got you elected mayor now, and I'm mighty proud of you and I need some help."

"All right, Grant, I'll be glad to help. I'll send you a check for twenty dollars. That all right?"

"Yes, sir, Mr. Ivan, that'll do nicely."

I had refinanced my campaign that morning and put in an additional $2,500 of my own money to pay up whatever loose bills were still owed, and there seemed to be no reason why I shouldn't give twenty dollars to Grant Carter. I had just been through a long campaign and many expenditures, the campaign was over, and I was very happy and anxious to be generous, and another twenty-dollar check didn't mean anything to me. Mills Lane, my campaign treasurer, sent Grant the check that afternoon.

When Grant got the check the next morning he was in no hurry to cash it. As it was a beautiful fall day, he sat on the front porch of his little house and flashed the check at anybody who came along. He was making himself out to be a close associate of the new mayor, Mr. Ivan Allen, Jr., and here was a gift from the mayor to prove it. Grant Carter was, I suspect, a very big man on his block that morning. But then a white "policy man"—an insurance agent who collects money door-to-door on a weekly basis from the black people—came by, making his rounds, and when he overheard Grant boasting about the check he immediately went to a phone and called Lester Maddox. Not an hour later somebody was there on Grant Carter's porch offering him thirty dollars for the twenty-dollar check made out on the Ivan Allen campaign account and signed by Mills B. Lane. Grant thought it was a good deal, since he had gotten enough mileage out of my check already. He traded checks.

When I came back to Atlanta several days later, the assistant foreman of the grand jury said he needed to talk to me immediately. He came by my office, greatly concerned, and explained that Maddox had appeared before the grand jury and accused me of buying Negro votes and submitted as evidence the check for twenty dollars. All I could do was laugh. "If you want to indict me," I said, "you'd better go ahead and indict half the people in Atlanta." Soon both of us were having a good laugh over the incident, and I thought that was the end of it.

But that twenty-dollar check still had a little mischief left in it. The next fall there was a heated race for governor between Carl Sanders and Marvin Griffin, and at a rally one night in Winder, Georgia, Griffin announced he was going to prove that "that Atlanta crowd Carl Sanders is tied up with"—Atlanta Newspapers, Ivan Allen, and Mills Lane—had been buying Negro votes. He had printed 10,000 facsimile copies of that check on check paper, with *Specimen* stamped on it, and after making the charge he threw the checks out over the crowd with a great flourish. They weren't *that* foolish, of course, and Griffin's act went over like a lead balloon. They weren't that dumb, either. Some of the people endorsed the "checks" and thirty-six of them cleared before the C&S Bank's expensive new electronic equipment could find the error. Marvin Griffin always was good at looking out for the tiny rural counties in Georgia at the expense of the bigger cities—stealing from the rich and giving to the poor is how he looked at it —and he enriched this one with $720 of Atlanta money that we never saw again.

# Learning the Ropes

Never do anything wrong that they can take a picture of.

—Mayor Emeritus William B. Hartsfield

When I moved into the mayor's office in January 1962, it was obvious that Atlanta and Georgia and the rest of the South had come to the crossroads; that a time of dynamic change lay ahead of us, and that we had to choose whether we wanted to fight change and drag along as we had always done in the South or accept the opportunity to grow with the rest of the country. At the bottom of everything at that time, of course, was the race issue: Atlanta public schools were to undergo more than token desegregation in September of that year, and we would not survive if we didn't cope with it. But there were other problems to be faced, because the Forward Atlanta program had already touched off the beginnings of the tremendous growth we would experience during the sixties. We had to lay the groundwork for a rapid-transit system. We had to plunge into urban renewal so that we could bring life back to the downtown area. We needed to upgrade our cultural, sports, and entertainment facilities. Our metropolitan population had gone over one million now, and it was time to raise our sights a little. It had been one thing to govern the Atlanta of the forties and fifties, as William B. Hartsfield had done so well, but it would be another matter dealing with the Atlanta of the sixties. The electric years were ahead of us.

Basically, the program I was pushing was the Six-Point Program I had conceived as president of the Chamber of Commerce. I had seen that planning followed up by hard work could make you a success in business, and was naïve enough to believe the same simple formula was all that you needed to be a success at City Hall. I figured if the aldermen and department heads continued to look after details, and were joined by the philanthropic civic leadership of the business community, there would be no real sweat being mayor of the city. My inaugural address—the shortest annual message I delivered to the board of aldermen in eight years—emphasized the need for more participation on the part of the business community:

Let me state here and now that I think the first rule of thumb for any of the things that must be done in Atlanta is this: that in any area where private enterprise can and will undertake a project, this must be done. This must be encouraged and endorsed and expected. Your city administration will enter the picture only when it has determined that private enterprise cannot undertake those services and provide those facilities which Atlanta must have . . .

Atlanta has by its reputation become one of the legends of the South and of the nation, a legend of progressiveness and a legend of what happens to a city that is determined to move forward in the direction of progress. We are a legend that has become real in our own lifetime. This is one of our greatest assets. This asset we have inherited and this asset we must not lose . . .

I have a growing belief that this new era we are entering into will be one in which people will look to their city government in many ways and for many things, but I have a profound conviction that this will be, and must be, an administration where there will be an increasing effort on the part of the city government to look to the citizens for more and more participation in areas where the city government does not reach . . .

I say that we begin now to build a tradition of citizen participation in Atlanta and that we build this tradition so that it becomes a part of the heritage of every child who is born in Atlanta and every child who moves to Atlanta . . .

Eight years later, when it was all over, it turned out that Atlanta *had* gained a reputation as a city whose business and civic leaders unselfishly offered their time and money and talent to make their city a better one. But it wasn't all that simple. I discovered very quickly that running a city isn't as cut-and-dried as running an office-equipment company; that it is one thing to make campaign promises and quite another thing to harness a massive city-government machine to make the promises come true. I simply was not conversant with the urban political process, having had little or no worthwhile experience at it. I didn't know how to push the buttons to get things going. I didn't know how to manipulate the board of aldermen. I didn't understand the very basic theory that the public has to be fully informed about what the city is doing or planning to do—through the use of citizens' advisory committees or through useful manipulation of the press—before you can gain its support. I had not gained the instinctive feel you have to have to do the right thing at the right time without having to sit down and think it over. This is something that can only come with experience on the job. (There is a story about a young man who takes over a high executive's position when the latter, highly respected for his ability to make snap decisions, retires. The young executive tries to emulate his predecessor, but fouls up every time. Finally, in desperation, he calls on the older man and asks him, "How the devil do you learn to make good snap decisions?" He is told, "By making *bad* snap decisions.") In short, I had to learn that one man can't get the job done by himself and that city government is a very big piece of machinery you do not operate with a mere snap of the fingers.

I got an inkling of what was in store for me on the night of the inauguration ceremonies when Louise and I drove up to the City Hall parking lot and were stopped by the attendant at the gate. "Buddy, I'm full up," he said. "Maybe you can find a place down there back of that church."

One thing I knew I had to have if I were ever going to be able to function in the mayor's office was a totally reliable and loyal staff. Hartsfield had been pretty much a loner during his two dozen years at City Hall (which a mayor of Atlanta could afford to be in those days), and much of the day-to-day operation of the city was done by the very excellent department heads, all of whom I inherited from the Hartsfield era. So I started from scratch as far as personal aides was concerned. For my secretary— and she became much more than merely a secretary during the next eight years—I brought with me from the Ivan Allen Company Ann Moses, a highly intelligent and articulate woman who had strong connections with the black community and had been a fine organizer of young people during the campaign.

As a sort of right-hand man I picked Captain George

Royal, one of the two city policemen I had hired to protect my son during the campaign, and George after six months with me could get things done faster than anybody at City Hall: he handled all telephone complaints, drove me around town, gave me an ear if I was grouchy, served as liaison man between my office and that of Police Chief Herbert Jenkins, and was more or less my troubleshooter.

And it was not until early 1964 that I finally talked Earl Landers into coming in as my administrative assistant, which was one of the smartest things I did as mayor. I hadn't been able to develop the type of administrative help I needed, and for two years I tried to get Landers to leave his job as city comptroller. At that time he had thirty-four years of experience in city government and was probably the most completely liked and highly respected person in city government—a man who had given to the city the same dedication that most people give to their own personal interests, and who looked after the city's tax money with the same diligence that most of us give our private bank accounts. He was totally dedicated, totally capable and totally committed to working behind the scenes—the perfect type of man a green mayor needs to help him pull the proper strings. Finally he said he would come as my administrative assistant, but he had a request. "Promise me there are two things you'll never ask me to do," he said. "One, I won't make speeches. Two, I won't get involved in any racial issues. I'm not suited for either." I agreed in a minute.

Generally speaking, though, my first year in office turned out to be a nightmare. Except in the field of civil rights, I accomplished very little. The city continued to grow on its own. I managed to put all city employees on a forty-hour week, and we talked the state legislature into a compromise agreement that provided for a commission to study rapid transit possibilities. But in general it was a time for me to learn how to be a mayor, a time for me to adjust myself to some of the fundamental facts of governmental life. When I went into office, for example, I knew we were going to have to raise the policemen's pitiful wages. A number of experts on the subject had told me that Atlanta was way out of line with other cities on that count, and I called a meeting of the finance committee and proposed that we provide a two-step pay increase for policemen. Fine, they said, but if you're going to give the police a raise you've got to give the firemen a raise. I soon learned that it is almost a tradition in the United States that if a policeman gets a raise so does a fireman, regardless of the comparative dangers and hours involved in the two jobs. Then I started hearing from people who said if we were going to raise the firemen and policemen we would have to raise all other city employees, which is what we finally had to do, financing a two-step raise for the 7,000 or so people who worked for the city just to do something about the disgracefully low pay for Atlanta's 900-odd policemen.

The worst setback I suffered during that first year was the resounding defeat of my proposed $80 million bond issue. The program I was pushing required the passing of a major bond issue. There were plans for the schools, roads, sewers, a civic center and auditorium, rapid transit; even a $9 million redevelopment plan which would turn Piedmont Park into the most beautiful in-town municipal park in the South. I understood the importance and the crying need for all of these things. There wasn't any doubt in my mind that the city needed them. There wasn't any doubt in my mind that the city could pay for them. There wasn't any doubt in my mind that we were on the threshold of great progress, and that now was the time to step out in high gear with a solid bond issue.

But what I didn't understand was the fact that the general public isn't as well versed on these subjects as those—like the mayor—who live in the center of the storm and have all of the facts at hand. I simply failed to communicate with the voters and with the board of aldermen on the bond issue. For example, the plan for the beautification of Piedmont Park suddenly blew up in my face and became a raging racial issue. The Woodruff Foundation had offered a gift of $4 million on the project, but as always asked that it be an anonymous gift. The redneck elements started screaming that the Piedmont Park plan was really an effort to integrate the park (it had already been integrated, but they failed to mention that), and that the $4 million anonymous gift was "nigger money." We had no defense because we couldn't announce that the Woodruff Foundation had offered to put up the money. The basic problem was, I had not educated the voters to the point that they fully understood what we were trying to do on the park project. The bond issue was beaten by a two-to-one vote. I suspected that the general public enjoys chastising a newly elected official on at least one occasion, just to let him know he won't always be able to have whatever he wants. I had to share some of the blame, too, owing to my failure to completely sell the urgent need for the bond issue. So I created a Citizen's Bond Study Commission (headed by Ed Smith of the First National Bank), to look into the causes of the defeat and make recommendations for another bond issue. The next year, then, after the need for a bond issue had been in the news for several months, a much smaller one ($39 million) passed in a breeze.

I even managed to lose what had been overwhelming support in the black community through my mishandling of another disaster that first year, the Peyton Road block-busting issue. There was a very nice white subdivision off

Peyton Road, on the southwest side of Atlanta, called Peyton Forest. The developer of the subdivision became dissatisfied with the rate of development there and made some threats to people in the area (he felt that they were standing in the way of his developing the land), pointing out that Negroes were moving into adjoining neighborhoods, and he just might start selling to them in Peyton Forest. The residents became indignant toward the developer and frightened about the encroachment of blacks on the area, and a volatile situation began to build up. It was the classic situation of a neighborhood being faced with racial transition. This took place in fifty-two separate formerly white neighborhoods in Atlanta during that one year, and often the situation was inflamed by "blockbusting" realtors and developers.

When I was advised of what was happening, I looked into the matter and saw that just north of Peyton Forest there were some eight hundred acres of unused land that had been improperly zoned commercial. Over the years it had been fairly common practice for the board of aldermen to create a buffer zone—a no-man's-land—between black and white neighborhoods by simply zoning a large enough area for commercial use. The result was, Atlanta city maps were dotted with scores of these unused plots of land. And this was at a time when we needed all the good land we could find for housing. So when the developer finally sold his own home in Peyton Forest to a prominent Negro doctor, setting off a holocaust among the whites there, I promptly decided to close off the subdivision—entrenched whites on one side, encroaching blacks on the other—with a barrier on Peyton Road. I saw it as a way of accomplishing two things: calming the white people in the neighborhood and focusing attention on the unused eight hundred acres so we could get it rezoned and put to use for low- or middle-priced housing. I saw it as a happy compromise between two very serious problems, and thought maybe I could be Solomon before it was over. But what I learned, once again, was that when you're dealing with the public you cannot assume they know all that you know. The people of Atlanta didn't understand all of the subtleties of the situation. They only saw a crude barricade—the "Atlanta Wall," it came to be called—stretched across a road, making a dividing line between whites and blacks. I had forgotten an axiom that William B. Hartsfield once used: "Never do anything wrong that they can take a picture of." The press had a heyday, and the feeling against me was understandably bitter in the Negro community. "I don't see how any decent white man can do what you have done," said the Reverend Sam Williams, who had been one of my stronger supporters in the past.

There was nothing much I could do then but try to weather the storm. I had not gotten my message over to the public, I had not sought sufficient advice on the thing, and I was completely in error in trying to solve the issue in such a crude way. National pressure was fierce: questions began to arise about Atlanta's image as a "City Too Busy to Hate," and we got word that while the issue raged at least two national magazines very nearly pulled upcoming stories on Atlanta. It was the courts that saved me in the end, declaring the barrier illegal after it had stood on Peyton Road for a couple of months. The day the court was supposed to render a decision I had a crew standing by at the barricade waiting for the final word, and when they were radioed the order they completely removed all signs of it in less than twenty minutes. When the press photographers and television crews got to Peyton Road, there was nothing there. I learned that Mayor Hartsfield had made a very good point.

If the failure of the bond issue and the blunder on Peyton Road hadn't been enough bad news for me in 1962, there was still more suffering—and this was a more personal and deeper anguish. On a beautiful Sunday morning in June I was rummaging around our farm at Franklin, Georgia, about seventy miles west of Atlanta near the Alabama line, when I was told that my wife had been trying to reach me by phone. I returned the call, and Louise said King Elliott, a newsman at WSB, had called with a fragmentary news report that a large number of Atlantans had been killed in the crash of a chartered jet plane at Orly Field in Paris. The news hit me like a Mack truck. Exactly a month earlier I had officially said good-bye to a group of 106 prominent Atlantans, most of them patrons of the arts who were visiting European art capitals under the sponsorship of the Atlanta Art Association. This was about the day they were supposed to return from Paris on Air France. If these early news reports were true, Atlanta was about to go through its greatest personal tragedy since General Sherman's visit.

I immediately called Ann Moses and told her to open the office and try to get something official, especially the list of Atlanta passengers, from Air France. Still wearing the old khakis I had been wearing around the farm, I jumped into my car and pointed it toward City Hall. As I sped toward the city I listened to the radio reports, which were still incomplete. At one point it was announced that my good friend Jack Glenn was on the plane, but I had been with Jack only a few days earlier and I knew better. Yet there was enough solid information now to make me certain that this was the Atlanta Art Association charter flight that had crashed, killing 106 Atlantans.

As they began to announce more names of those who were supposed to have been on the flight, my heart sank. I hadn't realized so many of my close, personal friends had made the trip. Dell Page . . . Tom Chris Allen . . . Morris and Martha Brandon . . . Nancy and Bob Pegram . . . Louise and Robby Robinson. The first date I ever had was with Nancy Frederick, later Mrs. Robert Pegram. One of my heaviest courtships during college days was with Louise Calhoun, later Mrs. Robby Robinson. These were my lifelong friends. This was my generation. This was also the backbone of Atlanta's cultural society, the city's leading patrons of the arts. There was no precedent for this kind of agony.

By the time I reached City Hall, having driven the seventy miles in slightly more than one hour, my office was a madhouse. Phones were ringing off the hook. Distraught relatives of people who were supposed to be on the flight didn't know where to turn. The networks and wire services were already calling and preparing to send people down to Atlanta. Local reporters and photographers surged back and forth in the office, which they were using as a nerve center on the disaster story, wanting to know what the city government was going to do. Still unshaven and wearing my khaki work clothes, I told them we would take all of the courtesy actions possible—issue a proclamation of sorrow, lower the flag at City Hall, assure the relatives that the city would offer any assistance necessary—but I knew this wasn't enough.

Finally I reached Gene Patterson, the only executive of Atlanta Newspapers whom I could locate on a Sunday morning, and when he asked me what I planned to do I surprised both of us by blurting out, "I'm going straight to Paris." Exactly what I could do when I got there, I hadn't considered. "That's the right thing to do," Patterson said. "You can at least represent those families over there." Just *how* I could represent them, I didn't know. But my instincts told me I should go.

It's one thing to say you're leaving immediately for Paris, and another thing to do it. Here it was, a Sunday morning, and I had to have airline tickets, cash, clothes, legal advice, shots, and a passport. We booked passage on the first

New York-to-Paris flight available that evening (it happened to be an Air France Boeing 707, the very same type of plane that had crashed at Orly that morning, something that didn't concern me but captured the fancy of the press). Fortunately I had a current passport and $1,500 cash in a safe-deposit box at Ivan Allen Company, two things I always kept on hand in case my parents were out of the country and needed me in a hurry because of illness or an accident. The city attorney couldn't be reached, and one of his associates who was leery of airplanes asked to be excused from flying over the Atlantic, but I finally got another associate city attorney, my old friend Edwin Sterne, to accompany me to Paris. When I couldn't locate either Senator Herman Talmadge or Senator Richard Russell, I asked Ann Moses to see if she could rouse anyone in the State Department who could help us in an emergency. I wondered what kind of action we were going to get from that great bureaucracy, and our prayers were answered: a young lady had been waiting for us to call and had taken care of everything—no shots, no passports, and "when you arrive in Paris you will be met by the American Embassy and any funds you require will be made available to you."

After hurriedly finishing some radio and television interviews and releasing a proclamation at City Hall, I rushed home to change clothes and throw some things in a suitcase, and then Louise drove me to the airport. Edwin Sterne was already there, ready to go, and Leonard Reinsch and Elmo Ellis of WSB had brought along Aubrey Morris, a man I respected as one of the finest radio newsmen I had ever known, who would, at WSB's expense, accompany me primarily as my press spokesman and secondarily as a WSB reporter. I had my money out, ready to pay for tourist-class seats to Paris (I always flew tourist when the city's money was involved), when an Air France official came up to me and said he had three com-

plimentary first-class round-trip tickets for us between
New York and Paris. Well, we didn't know whose fault the
accident at Orly was or what position the city might have
to take later on, so Edwin Sterne began earning his pay
right away: we would accept the courtesy tickets and save
the city's money, Edwin said, with the understanding that
we could pay for them if a conflict developed. It hadn't
been easy, getting on a plane headed for Paris, but we had
the difficult part ahead of us.

When we arrived in New York, to change planes for the
overseas flight, some thirty-five or forty newsmen and photographers were already waiting for us. New York newsmen
are a breed I was unaccustomed to handling, of course, and
it was apparent by their questions that they were trying
to goad me into making statements critical of Air France.
I had absolutely no information about the cause of the
crash and had no intention of getting into something like
that until I did. Aubrey Morris, a "good ol' boy" who can
get in there and punch with the best of them, handled his
peers as handsomely as possible, and we boarded the plane
for Paris. The responsibilities were bearing down on me so,
I didn't get a wink of sleep that night. Much of the night
was spent talking over legal aspects with Sterne, who told
me that I had absolutely no authority outside the city limits of Atlanta; the only way I could get anything done
would be through the sympathetic understanding of the
French government.

The instant the plane came to a stop on the ground at
Orly Field, the door was opened and two French gen-
darmes boarded the plane. "No one will leave the plane until Mayor Allen and his party have departed," one of them
said. It took no more for me to realize that the French, with
their compassion for man and their love of art, were pour-
ing out their hearts to Atlanta. As I stepped out of the cabin
onto the steps leading from the plane I couldn't believe my

eyes. Spread out below me at the foot of the steps, wearing striped trousers and frock coats on a beautiful hot June morning in Paris, were more than two dozen members of the official French family: a personal representative of Charles de Gaulle, the head of French aviation, chairman of the board of Air France, *et al.* I realized how insignificant I was, but I knew I had to assume the posture of representing these families and, indeed, the entire city of Atlanta, Georgia. I knew nothing about protocol, foreign relations, aviation, international agreements, or any of the other details I might become involved in. I was nothing but the mayor of Atlanta and a friend and neighbor of 106 people who had been killed at this same airport only the day before. All I could think was, *At least you've got a good education and at least some training, and what if Lester Maddox had become mayor instead of you?* There would be several other occasions in the next eight years that I would feel the spotlight on me, but this was the first time. As I walked down the steps to meet this delegation I threw my shoulders back and sucked in my stomach and talked myself into summoning all of the dignity and restraint I could find. I would represent those families to the best of my ability.

I have never met with a more understanding and sympathetic group. They were anxious to help in any way, and after the usual exchange of greetings and extensions of sympathy it was suggested that I hold a press conference. Instead of the half-dozen reporters I was accustomed to talking to at press conferences in Atlanta, or the thirty-five or forty who had met us in New York, there were about 150 at Orly—international press, local reporters, the wire services, photographers, television cameramen, and broadcasters—the largest contingent of newsmen I was to meet during my years in office. I spoke no French at all, and again I was being maneuvered into a position of indicting Air France for the crash, but somehow the press conference came off well. Then everybody moved to the scene of the accident.

It is difficult to describe the feeling I had as we looked through the charred wreckage. Only twenty-four hours earlier this huge droop-winged plane had roared down the runway, headed back to Atlanta with intimate friends of mine aboard. They had spent a month happily touring the art centers of Europe, had gathered valuable insights and ideas on what could be done to expand Atlanta's culture, and had bought many expensive paintings, artifacts, and souvenirs to take back home for themselves or for friends. Trouble had developed as soon as the Boeing 707 was beginning to roll, and the pilot decided to abort takeoff by locking the wheels. The tires wore off, and then the rims. A tremendous amount of static electricity was building up as the plane slithered off the end of the runway. It clipped a couple of telephone poles, bounced across a narrow access road, slid another thousand feet on its belly and finally slammed into a small stone cottage, which spun it around and broke the tail section free, saving the lives of three stewardesses. Of the 127 persons aboard, those three were the only ones to live.

And now, the morning after the crash, we were being shown where the wheels had locked and skid marks had dug into the concrete for some eleven hundred feet. The fuselage looked like the burned-out skeleton of a whale, the ribbed tail section hovering over it like a vulture. And all over the area, scattered for hundreds of yards, there were the personal belongings of my friends. I recognized some of the pastel tulle dresses that Nancy Frederick, my first date, always wore and looked so beautiful in. I saw bottles of rare champagne, bought on the trip, which had miraculously survived when the baggage compartment was thrown clear. I picked up a West Point Rotary Club flag, which belonged to my friend Morgan Canty, and got permission to take it back with me and give to the club. It was a gruesome task, having to walk through the wreckage and discover so many belongings of close friends, but I had to get a clear understanding of how the accident happened so that I could be prepared for the inevitable questions that heartbroken families and friends would ask me when I returned to Atlanta.

Then, after lunch in Paris, we had to go to the morgues to try to identify the bodies. We were joined by another friend, Harvey Hill, who had flown to Paris because his best friend, Robby Robinson, had been on the plane. The bodies were in five separate morgues. The bodies were not defaced, and in most cases the hair had not been burned off, but there had been a terrible fire that had browned the skin just enough to make it impossible to identify anyone. The closest we came to making any identification was by a bracelet on one body and a checkbook in the pocket of another. We gratefully returned to our hotel and made some thirty transatlantic calls that night, to the press and to relatives of those who had been killed, trying in some way to console them and explain what had happened and assure them that Air France and the French government were doing everything possible as far as identification and return of the bodies was concerned.

The following morning, which was a Tuesday, we had our only chance to smile a little when Aubrey Morris temporarily abandoned his role as a public-relations officer and went back to being a reporter. Aubrey had quite a reputation in Atlanta as a persistent seeker of facts. One story they tell is about the time some Georgia official was trying to lay low on a sticky issue, and said to Aubrey, "I have no comment on that." Aubrey jammed the microphone in his face and said, "Well, sir, if you *had* a comment what would it be?" And I'll be damned if the politician didn't tell him, on the air. Anyway, that morning we went by to see Jim Gavin, the former paratroop commander who was then U.S. ambassador to France. Gavin and I stopped in the middle of a conversation in his elegant office when we saw Aubrey calmly reach for a phone on the ambassador's desk, punch a button that said DIRECT LINE WASHINGTON, and say, "Give me WSB radio in Atlanta, Georgia, please." The White House operator began to put him through. Gavin's stern military and foreign-protocol background hadn't prepared him for Aubrey Morris, and he was frantically punching buttons to summon press secretaries and attachés. Before he could get guidance, he had already given Aubrey an interview over his own phone to Atlanta.

There wasn't much else for us to do in Paris. On Wednesday morning a magnificent memorial service, attended by hundreds of Americans and scores of Parisians, was held in the American Cathedral. Gene Patterson had arrived by this time for a newspaper publishers' convention, and he helped us make the final arrangements with Air France to send a delegation to Atlanta to explain about the crash and the plans for the transferral of the bodies. When we got back to Atlanta that night and were met by a large crowd of citizens and newsmen, it was only the beginning of long and sad hours of reconstructing everything we knew about the accident. There was no widespread anger toward Air France, only an empty sadness over the loss of so many of our finest leaders in one flaming instant. Atlanta did manage, however, to turn its adversity into success. That crash served as the catalyst for the building of the $13 million Atlanta Memorial Arts Center, a stunning memorial to the 106 Atlantans who went to Europe for knowledge and never came back.

# The Race Issue

Thank goodness for Birmingham and Alabama. If America survives, Alabama must be given much of the credit . . . Just remember, FREE DESSERT for Mothers on Mother's Day . . .

—Newspaper ad for Lester Maddox's Pickrick Restaurant, 1963

When I decided during my campaign that the real issue for Atlanta was the race issue, I didn't know then just how correct I was. From the time I walked into City Hall in January 1962 until the passage of the Civil Rights Act in 1964, I was deeply involved day after day and hour after hour in trying to solve racial problems. There was simply no end to it. Civil rights was the big national issue, and it was becoming an even bigger issue in our city. This is not hard to understand when you realize that we were in the center of one of the four hard-core segregated states—Georgia, Ala-

81

bama, Mississippi, and South Carolina—where there were more blacks, where there were more white racists, where the problem had started in the first place, where feelings were more intense on both sides of the fight. Being the melting pot of the Southeast, Atlanta in the early sixties possessed all of the elements that could lead to full-scale racial bloodshed and turmoil: headquarters for the civil-rights organizations and white-racist groups alike, half-white and half-black in the city limits, an abundance of old-school segregationist politicians like Lester Maddox, a growing school of impatient young blacks such as Stokely Carmichael. Consequently, I was never far away from my next race issue. There would be what I call "indignation meetings" of white neighborhood associations, demanding a hearing and telling me Negroes had moved onto their block and asking what the city was going to do about it, adding that they had fought in the world wars and if the city didn't do something about protecting their hard-earned homes they would take matters into their own hands. There would be picketing from black students demanding to be allowed to eat in certain restaurants, and outraged cries from the restaurateurs themselves. There would be visits from out-of-town blacks who had been denied access to a hotel, followed by outright threats from the hotel owner if my reaction was not to his liking.

Atlanta was still almost totally segregated when I became mayor in 1962. There had been some progress made in the two preceding years, but most of it was insignificant. The buses had been desegregated, along with the golf courses and, to some extent, the parks. Some desegregation had taken place, of course, in the area of downtown hotels and restaurants and department stores. Under the influence of Fred Storey of the Storey theater chain, owners of movie houses were leaning toward desegregating their places. And, too, token desegregation had taken place in some public schools in September 1961. But, generally speaking, Atlanta was a tightly segregated city when I took over, and City Hall itself was one of the most segregated buildings in the state of Georgia: separate drinking fountains and restrooms, separate employment listings, segregated use of the City Hall cafeteria, even an ordinance that said Negro policemen (there were 48 of them on the 900-man force) could not arrest whites.

There was an expectation on the part of the citizens of Atlanta (to the delight of some, to the disdain of most) that when I became mayor I would work miracles in civil rights. I had been, after all, the "liberal" candidate and had swamped Lester Maddox with the aid of nearly all of the black votes cast. Exactly how I would go about "solving" the racial issue, I didn't know. We simply didn't know enough about the problem at that time, and when I say "we" I'm including the leaders of the black community, who knew as little as the white leaders did about precisely what moves would have to be made in order to break down the barriers of segregation in the city. I had never outlined to the Negro people, in perhaps a hundred different rallies and meetings, any specifics. I had only talked about segregation in vague terms, saying that I hoped during my years in office that I would be able to eliminate racial prejudice and that I would like to see a world in which the word "race" was eliminated. I would praise the Emancipation Proclamation and speak of America as a nation of crusades, but I never attempted to define exactly *how* I would handle hotel problems or open the swimming pools to everyone or see that a Negro could eat in any restaurant he chose. This great issue of desegregation in America had been simmering since the school desegregation ruling by the Supreme Court in 1954, and still there were few leaders in the country who knew how to go about solving it. And now the issue was beginning to boil. When I received

10,000 replies to the lengthy questionnaire I mailed out to all registered voters during the campaign, asking what they thought the major issues were and what could be done about them, the overwhelming majority listed the racial issue as the leading problem to be faced ("Run Martin Luther King back to Africa" was about as learned as the suggestions came).

One thing I knew, since I was committed to easing racial tensions and bringing about more racial equality, I could start there at City Hall. I'm not taking away from William Hartsfield when I say it was tightly segregated, because he was a liberal in his time just as I will probably be called a liberal in my time. He understood the problem and met it as a man concerned with his times, but the whole issue of civil rights didn't come into focus until just as he was leaving office. So when I went into the mayor's office there was still a double standard in City Hall itself, and J. H. Calhoun, representing the black community, gave me a mimeographed sheet listing some conditions that the Negro people would like me to consider. The list included the elimination of separate drinking fountains and separate restrooms in City Hall, the hiring of Negro firemen, the right of arrest of whites for Negro policemen, the elimination of the dual employment register in city government. This seemed to be the extent of the hopes and aspirations of the Negro people at the time.

The first day I was in office, I gave out instructions to take down all the signs in the building designating "white" and "colored." Then I called together the five or six major department heads, shortly after eliminating the practice of having separate listings for black and white prospective city employees, and told them in certain terms what I expected of them. "I hold every one of you in high regard," I said, "but I'm making it plain to you that you're not going to be reappointed unless you do a better job in the field of Negro employment."

The whole thing changed after that. We had already hired some Negro firemen (for stations in Negro sections) and given Negro policemen the power to arrest whites, but soon we were quickly stepping out ahead of every other city in the South as far as hiring Negroes for other than the most menial jobs was concerned. And I was being "blamed" for it, of course, by a considerable segment of the white population. On opening night of the Southern Association baseball season at old Ponce de Leon Park that first year in office, I was invited to throw out the first ball to launch the Atlanta Crackers' season. This was the first time there would be integrated seating at "Poncey," and the first time Negro players would appear in the league. Birmingham, a rabid baseball town and for years Atlanta's hated rival, had dropped out of the league rather than play integrated baseball. As we didn't intend to sacrifice our baseball team over the race issue we went ahead as though nothing had changed. When I was announced over the public address system and prepared to throw out the first ball, my ears burned from a loud chorus of boos. I wanted to ask them what they wanted the most: to hate Negroes or to watch baseball.

I was learning that the best way for me to handle a racial problem was by barging into it myself, since somebody would always wind up throwing it right back into my lap anyway, and there seemed to be no satisfactory intermediaries. I had reached that point in my thinking on the race issue when George Royal came into my office one September afternoon in 1962 and said a problem had come up in the cafeteria located in the basement of City Hall. Technically, the cafeteria was for all city employees or their guests; but in practice the few Negroes who worked in City Hall simply didn't go in there except to pick up a

sandwich or a cup of coffee. It had never been tested. It
was just one of those unspoken rules, that the cafeteria
was for whites only. Anyway, Royal told me that Mrs.
Prudence Herndon, a prominent Negro lawyer in town,
had gone into the cafeteria with nine Atlanta University
students—boys and girls, black and white—and they were
refused service. Mrs. Herndon and I were good friends,
she being an associate of Judge A. T. Walden, and I told
Royal I would handle the situation myself.

Mrs. Herndon and the students were cooling their heels
in the lobby of City Hall when I found them. "Mrs. Herndon," I said, "do you have a problem?"

"Yes, Mayor, I do," she said. "They won't let us eat."

"You understand what the ordinances say, that only city
employees and their guests can go into the cafeteria?"

"Yes, but I think there was another reason."

"So do I. What can we do?"

"I would prefer that you handle it."

"Okay. I'm inviting you to be my guests."

As we walked down the steps to the cafeteria, I won-
dered what I was getting myself into. Here you are, I
thought, a new mayor with seven or eight thousand city
employees, trying to make your way, trying to gain their
support, trying to gain their favor, wanting to be friendly,
wanting to build an organization. And now you are getting
ready to lead a confrontation against them on the testiest
issue they have: eating with black people.

We reached the cafeteria during the afternoon coffee
break, and about a hundred employees, all of them white,
were sitting at the tables. At the sight of the new mayor
coming in with nine black and white students, they fell
silent and watched every move we made. The white wait-
ress behind the counter was flustered.

"I want you to serve my guests," I told her.

She recovered quickly. "I'm not going to do it."

"I said these are my *guests*. I want you to serve them."

"I won't do it, Mayor."

"Then come out from behind there, and *I'll* serve them."

"If you put it that way," she said, "I'll do it."

I thought I had it made for a few minutes. When we had all been served cool drinks we walked toward some tables and took seats. At that instant, every single person in that cafeteria got up and walked out. I tried to carry on a conversation with the students, but my heart wasn't in it. *Well, you've blown it now,* I thought. Then, to my amazement, every one of the employees came right back into the cafeteria and took their seats again. What had happened was, I learned later, when they had gone outside and were standing around jabbering about what I had done, George Royal had swarmed over them like a mother hen. "You're a bunch of damned fools," he said, "giving up your cafeteria just because some young students want to cool off with a Coke." They saw what a farce it really was, hung their heads, and swallowed a little "pride" and came back. So much for the desegregation of the City Hall cafeteria.

There is no doubt in my mind that I was turning a little more liberal every day as a reaction against the totally irrational and irresponsible acts of the white racists around me. I wasn't so all-fired liberal when I first moved into City Hall, but when I saw what the race-baiters were doing or could do to hold back the orderly growth of Atlanta, it infuriated me and eventually swung me to the extreme end opposite them. It reached the point that I had absolutely no compassion and no patience with these people, and a good example of how I began to deal with them was the confrontation I had in 1963 with the manager of the Henry Grady Hotel.

The Henry Grady wasn't the finest hotel in the city by any means, but it had been a traditional meeting place and watering hole for many years for the more conservative politicians in the state when they came in for the general assembly each year. The manager at that time was a man by the name of Emory Crenshaw, who I am certain voted for Maddox. He was very much against the desegregation of public facilities of the Henry Grady Hotel in Atlanta, and had been blocking our attempts to open public accommodations in the city to Negroes.

That year we were holding endless meetings between black leaders and hotel operators in an attempt to solve the issue of hotel desegregation. After one of those meetings, I wrote a confidential letter to everybody on the committee (including Crenshaw, who had refused to attend), summing up some of the progress we had made and enclosing some information on how the city of Dallas had coped with its problems. The same letter went out to everybody, black and white, but each had a personal salutation. Three months later I heard that doctored copies of this letter—copies of the one that had been addressed to Dr. Miles Smith, president of the Atlanta chapter of the National Association for the Advancement of Colored People—were being circulated around town in an effort to kill the upcoming bond election. Some of the points in my letter had been edited out (especially a phrase indicating that everybody had gotten the same letter), and at the bottom of the letter was an addition: "Don't give the 'captive mayor' of the minority bloc a blank check to use against the other voters and taxpayers of Atlanta. Vote Against Bonds!" The implication was that here is a secret letter from Mayor Allen to the NAACP, which proves they are conspiring against the white people of Atlanta. I was enraged when I was shown a copy.

It didn't take me long to trace it back to Emory Crenshaw. He had gone by the convention bureau and asked to see the hotel desegregation committee files and had taken a copy of the letter addressed to Dr. Smith. I went by to get Walter Crawford, director of the convention bureau, and then we drove over to the Henry Grady. When we entered the hotel we saw Crenshaw in the lobby and approached him.

"Are you in?" I said.

"You see me, don't you?" he said.

"I want to see you now."

We went into his office and he closed the doors, and we got to the point in a hurry. I waved one of the doctored copies of the letter in his face and said, "I understand you did this."

"No, it was a group of interested citizens."

"Where did they get the letter?"

"All right, they got it from me. What about it?"

My blood pressure was boiling. "What about it? You know damned good and well what you've done. You're trying to kill the bond issue, and you're trying to make up another 'nigger problem' to do it. You were given a confidential letter as a gentleman, and you've misused it."

Crenshaw said, "Fine. Just so it works. I hope it crucifies the bond election and the whole city and everything else until City Hall gets in better hands."

And I blew my stack. We got into an impassioned name-calling contest. I said, "I hope you get what's coming to you." When I left the hotel, Crenshaw and I were still shouting at each other. The important thing is, however, that the press got hold of the story and played it up the next day. It was another of my early experiences of the fact that in trying to run a big city you have to get things out into the open and let the press know about them in order to get them clarified. The news story about my confrontation with Crenshaw ("Eyeball to Eyeball," Gene Patterson's column was entitled) killed whatever effect his bogus letter was having on the bond election.

By the end of the sixties, I felt Atlanta had coped with the race issue better than any other major city in America. When you consider the additional hurdles we had to jump —nearly fifty per cent black population, centered in the most segregated part of the country, hounded by racists —it was a fantastic accomplishment. In less than ten years we came from a situation in which a Negro policeman could not arrest a white person to a position of being one of the few big cities in the nation where a black man had a reasonable chance of getting a job, properly raising his family, enjoying the cultural benefits of his city, and having an audience for his complaints at City Hall. Certainly, there was still tension between the extreme factions in the black and white communities (we may never see the day when that ends), but this was far overshadowed by a growing understanding and respect between the moderate upper-middle classes of both races.

By the end of the sixties there was complete desegregation of all public facilities in Atlanta. There was a Negro vice-mayor. There were several Negro officers on the police force, and Negroes were beginning to qualify for and gain the better jobs in city government. There were black and white children studying side by side in most of the public schools, though "bussing" had become an issue, and the further desegregation of schools promised to be one of the major problems facing the new city administration. And in some areas black and white were living in the same neighborhoods, thanks to even-tempered white residents who saw that the real enemy was the unscrupulous "block-busting" realtor rather than the Negro neighbor. The society pages of the Atlanta newspapers were no longer reserved for white brides or white-party hostesses only. Hank Aaron was lustily cheered at Atlanta Stadium by fans who had been willing to drop out of the Southern Association at one point rather than give in to integrated baseball. This is not to say that Atlanta was Utopia for the black man. It was far from it. Lester Maddox was still in the Capitol, surrounded by scores of old-time Georgia demagogues still trying to turn back the clock to the nineteenth century. There was a frightening flight to the suburbs on the part of white residents worried about how "the nigger's takin' over." Some of the federal slum programs for which we had held so much hope—Model Cities, Economic Opportunity Atlanta, et al.—were showing too little in the way of meaningful progress, as was true in most of the nation. But Atlanta had gone through the sixties with only one major racial disturbance while most of the rest of the country had come through them with irreparable scars, and what we did in the field of racial progress had to be the major acomplishment of my administration.

There were many reasons why Atlanta managed the race issue while other cities like Birmingham in the South and Newark in the North fumbled around and nearly let it kill them. For one thing, Atlanta was one of the more sophisticated and cosmopolitan cities in the United States, in spite of its sleepy Southern façade, a city top-heavy with people who were well-educated white-collar workers and executives and had come there from all over and chosen to stay there because they loved Atlanta. For another reason, the city was economically sound—and social progress can be made only when there is economic progress. And I will not deny that some of my impetuous acts—leading the black students into the City Hall cafeteria, testifying in behalf of the Civil Rights Act in Washington, going to the side of Mrs. Martin Luther King, Jr., when her husband was shot—helped drag a sometimes reluctant white community toward racial understanding. But I think the most important factor in Atlanta's attempts to cope with the race issue during the sixties was the presence of a large established black community and a pragmatic white business "power structure." When you look around you will find that no other city of the sixties had, at the core of its economic and social base, black and white leaders who were so willing to understand each other and work with each other: to make recommendations, to make concessions, to make personal sacrifices, in order to accomplish the most good for the most people.

Our black community was not led by a handful of renegades intent upon selling out their own race or filling their personal coffers or demanding that an unfair system be overturned in a day; rather, they were well-educated, proud, sober people like the Reverend William Holmes Borders, the spiritual and economic leaders of their community, who were concerned with bettering the Negro's lot but willing to give us a little more time to learn.

Our white community was not led by bombastic, self-seeking politicians unwilling to budge an inch on the question of racial equality; rather, they were civic-minded, level-headed businessmen like Mills B. Lane, who knew that no city could be any stronger than its weakest link— the low-income Negro, in this case—and were willing to question the old ways of the South and to change. Nothing would have worked had not both sides been able to work together for a better Atlanta, which was the driving force for all of the leaders of Atlanta—black and white— during the sixties. I wish I had kept records on exactly how many times I arranged or refereed meetings of the black and white leaders in the city; meetings covering problems ranging from the desegregation of downtown department stores to preparations for the Martin Luther King, Jr., funeral; meetings held in a multitude of places from the Commerce Club to tiny offices on the campus of Atlanta University. It was the willingness of these leaders to sit down and talk things out that made Atlanta's transition from a bastion of segregation to an open city possible.

We of the "white-power structure" were particularly vulnerable, however, on one point: the continuing segregation of the Commerce Club and our own private social clubs. Although the Negro leaders demonstrated great patience on this matter, the militant young blacks and the more idealistic liberals in the city never let up on their charges that while it was true that we were making better racial progress in Atlanta than in any other city, our motives were not entirely honorable. "Look," the argument would go, "if Allen and Lane and those other fat cats are so liberal, why don't they let Negroes eat with them at the Commerce Club and the Piedmont Driving Club?" There was substance to the charge that the liberalism of the white business community was motivated purely by pragmatism—if Atlanta didn't solve its racial problems it would suffer economically just as Birmingham had—rather than by a genuine sympathy toward the suffering of the Negro.

Ironically, Lester Maddox hosted the first integrated dinner ever held at the Piedmont Driving Club. The Driving Club was *the* private club in the city, an historical and elegant old place to which the white upper crust had traditionally belonged for many years. My generation had inherited membership in the Piedmont Driving Club and others of that type, all of which had rigid unwritten rules against the admission of Negroes (and, in some cases, Jews), and as I began to gain a reputation as a civil-rights leader I became embarrassed about the situation; but decided rather than resigning from them I would stay in and see if I could change the rules from within when the time came. At any rate, one day there was a luncheon hosted by Governor Maddox and the state Department of Commerce in honor of one of the national magazines. When everybody sat down for lunch, I looked down the table and saw two black television newsmen from Atlanta station WAGA-TV. They were part of the luncheon party, just like everybody else. I watched with interest as the head waiter went rushing to the *maître d'*, who went for the assistant manager, who went for the manager. While they were all standing there wringing their hands in a terrible quandary, wondering what they were going to do, I turned to Don Elliott Heald of WSB and said, "If they attempt to move those two Negroes out of this dining room, I'm going to go out with them." Curiously, Maddox didn't seem to notice the two were there. Perhaps it just didn't seem worth the effort to try to maintain segregation any more, because finally the manager and his assistants just shrugged their shoulders and walked away without forcing a confrontation. The Piedmont Driving Club never did become a fortress of liberal thought, but by the end of the decade it was at least possible to take a black guest there.

It wasn't quite as easy to knock down the barriers at the Commerce Club, a private club atop the Commerce Building open to members of the Atlanta Chamber of Commerce and their guests. It had rules against serving Negroes, though I had broken those rules in 1961 by secretly meeting in some of the private back rooms with the black leaders during the sit-in crisis. However, the Commerce Club remained steadfastly segregated. There was a long history of abortive attempts to integrate the place. In my second year as mayor I had nearly $700 worth of engraved invitations printed for the annual dinner I was throwing for the state legislature (to promote harmony between the city and the state), but had forgotten that there was now a Negro in the legislature, Senator Leroy Johnson of Atlanta, and had to cancel the dinner because the Commerce Club wouldn't allow Senator Johnson through the door. This sort of thing kept happening, and somewhere around 1965 Mills Lane said to me, "Look, the issue of Negroes coming into the Commerce Club has been with us a long time, and we've never faced up to it. I know how you feel about it, so why don't you bring it up at the next meeting of the board?" The next meeting was a big one that included Robert Woodruff, three bank presidents, and some of the city's most prominent white business leaders—sixteen of them in all. Mills, in his usual offhand way, said, "Ivan has a matter that has been of concern to the club for a long time, and he wants to bring it up." I got up and said, "Gentlemen, let's don't beat around the bush. We can't dodge this issue the rest of our lives. This is the club of commerce, in which we've tried to cut across all lines in the city and bring the entire business community together. I'm making a motion that we accept Negro citizens as guests." There was dead silence. Sixteen were present, but I didn't get a second to my motion. Finally, Mr. Woodruff leaned over to me and said in an audible whisper, "Ivan, you're absolutely right." It was an eloquent testimony to the influence of Robert Woodruff over Atlanta's younger white business leaders. Hands began to fly up, signifying seconds, and the motion passed unanimously.

We were presented with a chance to cross the last racial barrier, throw aside the remnants of our old bigotry, when Dr. Martin Luther King, Jr., was awarded the Nobel Peace Prize in 1964. The Nobel committee had selected Dr. King as that year's recipient because of the leadership he had offered in the civil-rights fight for nearly a decade. He had been on the front lines from the very beginning, making tremendous personal sacrifices—being spat upon, cursed, jailed, and threatened with his life—because of his belief in the equality of men and his dedication to nonviolence. To most of the world he was being looked upon as a new Gandhi, and his selection for the award was generally well received. The reaction was different in much of the white South, of course. We had made great strides in civil rights in recent years, but we hadn't come *that* far. We still had more than our share of racists and bigots in Atlanta and the rest of the South, and not all of them were blue-collar Wallaceites living with their hatred and bitterness on the fringes of town. Many of these people made up the privileged Southern class: people who belong to the exclusive country clubs and work in air-conditioned skyscrapers and go home every evening to expensive lily-white suburbs so they can carry on their tirade against the Negro in smug isolation. There was still great bitterness inside the Southern business community toward Dr. King's successful efforts at desegregating public facilities. And so the awarding of the Nobel Peace Prize to him brought the haters out of the woodwork once more. "Martin Luther Coon," they were calling him. Rather than being called a great humanitarian, they were saying, he should be found guilty of treason. It seemed incredible that there would be this sort of response in his own town to a man who had been so honored, but that is the way it was.

By this time I had reached the point where I had total confidence in my actions and my feelings on the civil-rights issue. For nearly five years I had been deeply involved in working out our problems in Atlanta, and only a year earlier I had totally committed myself by going to Washington and testifying in behalf of President Kennedy's public accommodations bill before a Senate committee. So when word of Dr. King's selection came I instinctively began thinking about some way the city of Atlanta could honor him. A biracial banquet seemed to me to be the most appropriate way to do this. As far as I knew there had never been anything like that in Atlanta, not on a large official scale at least, and I was sure something like that would raise a furor. After firing off a congratulatory wire to Dr. King, in effect passing on official best wishes from the city of Atlanta, I started talking privately about a huge dinner to honor the Nobel Prize winner and sat back to see what would happen.

We went through several tumultuous weeks in the wake of the Nobel announcement. Not only were there strong debates in the truck stops and the all-night diners and the factories about King's selection, there was also resentment in the Atlanta business community. Again I found myself a half-step ahead of my friends on the race issue, dragging them along behind me. I was angry at some people who had been my friends for a long time, and I was beginning to think about how it was going to look if Martin Luther King, Jr., were not even recognized in his own city as a Nobel winner when Paul Austin, president of the Coca-Cola company, came up to me in the field during a hunting trip in south Georgia and said, "You're right. Dr. King has won the Nobel Prize, and the city should properly acknowledge it."

When we got back to Atlanta, Austin called a meeting of two dozen prominent white business leaders one night at the Piedmont Driving Club. There was general agreement at the meeting that there should be a biracial dinner, and that they would support it. I don't think you could say there was overwhelming, enthusiastic endorsement for the planned dinner. They were for it primarily on pragmatic grounds: that it would look bad for Atlanta's image if we did *not* honor Dr. King. I was asked to close the meeting by summing up what had been discussed, and some of my bitterness came out. "Well, gentlemen," I said, "I have listened to your reasons for support and I am sure I'll find that you will support it financially and that you will glory in the very fine national publicity that you will receive. But on the night of the banquet it's my guess that very few of you will be present. Most of you will be out of town or sick, and you'll send someone to represent you. Don't let it worry you, though. The mayor will be there."

I think this stirred their consciences a bit. Whatever the cause, almost every major white business leader in Atlanta was in attendance the night more than fifteen hundred blacks and whites gathered at the old Dinkler Hotel in the very center of downtown Atlanta to honor Dr. Martin Luther King, Jr. Understandably, there was tension in the hall where the banquet was being held. Out front, on the sidewalk, some members of the Ku Klux Klan were picketing. There had been a raft of bomb threats, and we had some two hundred plainclothesmen planted in the audience. Then, too, there was the natural uneasiness that would come at a first biracial gathering such as this. I had an opportunity to put everyone at ease, which I felt was my job, when those of us who would be at the head table were waiting in another room before entering the main dining hall. Somebody came up to the Reverend Sam Williams and me and apologized to us that the dinner was going to run about forty-five minutes late because of the unexpectedly large turnout. "Don't worry about that," I said. "My friend Sam Williams has been waiting for a hundred years to get in that ballroom, and forty-five minutes one way or the other isn't going to bother him much."

It was a wonderful occasion. The King children were in the peak of their youth, climbing on top of the table and under the table, getting all of the attention they could. I was seated next to Mrs. King, and as I talked to her I began to see the great depth and patience she had. Dr. King made a magnificent address, and I gave him a proclamation bound in a beautiful lavender velvet portfolio; probably the most handsome official gift the city presented while I was in office. The evening was also another chance for me to get to know Martin Luther King, Jr., a little better. Here he was, winner of the Nobel Prize, giving him every reason in the world to be somewhat bitter or pompous toward people who had spent much of their past lives fighting what he had dedicated his life to do. But he was a big man, a great man. He had arrived late for dinner, and I remember his leaning over and apologizing to me.

"I forgot what time we were on," he said with a grin.

"How's that?" I said.

"Eastern Standard Time, CST or CPT."

"CPT?"

"Colored People's Time," he said. "It always takes us longer to get where we're going."

# Washington

Unsigned letter: I wish to nominate you as
Mr. Mau Mau of 1963. I understand that you
are a half-brother of Martin Luther King.

New York Times editorial: On rare occasions
the oratorical fog on Capitol Hill is pierced by
a voice resonant with courage and dignity.

 —Reactions to Senate testimony in
  behalf of a public-accommodations bill

By the end of my first year in office, long before the historic dinner for Dr. King, I was probably as experienced in the civil-rights fight—and I mean experienced in combat, working on the myriad problems from day to day in the trenches—as any other major public official in the South, if not the nation. It is one matter to be a Congressman or a governor or even a state legislator and be able to isolate and protect yourself from the people and their problems, but it is something else to be a mayor and have to cope with crises every hour of every day on a direct lo-

100

cal level. A mayor is right on the scene, easily accessible, and the problems that come to him are immediate. There is, sadly, little time to theorize or pass the buck to a committee for study or otherwise put off until tomorrow what must be done today. So I had to claw and scratch my way through the civil-rights struggle and learn the hard way. There had been the incident in the cafeteria and the elimination of the Jim Crow signs at City Hall. There had been the question over the authority of Negro policemen to arrest whites. There had been the hiring of Negro firemen. There had been, for better or for worse, Peyton Road. I had wrestled almost daily with the desegregation of swimming pools, golf courses, movie houses, schools, restaurants, hotels, neighborhoods, restrooms, parks, water fountains, and almost every other public facility known to man. The leaders on both sides of the fight, from Lester Maddox to Martin Luther King, Jr., were not names signed to letters that were notated "FYI" and passed on to me by a large office staff. They were real people whom I knew intimately from sometimes frantic discussions on simmering sidewalks and in stuffy upstairs rooms and crowded ghetto front porches. I was beginning to feel that perhaps my father had understated the case about fifteen years earlier when he predicted that my generation would be confronted with "the greatest agony that any generation ever went through." God knows, for a mayor *agony* wasn't a strong enough word.

Predictably, because I was so closely involved in it all, the experiences of that first year had a great effect on my personal view of the entire issue of racial equality. As I have pointed out, my Southern background had left me with a blind spot as far as the needs and the conditions and the ambitions of the Negro were concerned. Until I entered the office there had been only very slow, subtle changes in my attitude—from absolutely no discussions of the racial issue while a student at Georgia Tech, to occasional outbursts when I would rant "nigger" at some black person I was somehow put out with, to the confrontations with Bertha Lewis and L. D. Milton during the Community Chest drive. I recall a time shortly after the Bertha Lewis incident when, as a young would-be civic leader, I told a group of Negro citizens that they should have a deep sense of appreciation for everything Mayor Hartsfield had done for them (it was a classic example of the same old paternalism of the South), and had the Reverend William Holmes Borders defiantly stroke my face with his finger and say, "Did anything rub off? Am I any different, or am I a man just like you?"

My liberalism was late in coming, but once I leaned in that direction I suppose I went all the way in a hurry. In that one year, that first year in office, I must have seen as much of the racial tension on both sides as most people would see in two lifetimes. Dealing with the problems at first hand, day by day, was the most important factor, of course. And there can't be any question about the effect it had on me to see Ralph McGill and Eugene Patterson of the *Atlanta Constitution* moving so vigorously and courageously into the civil-rights question. Then, too (I don't think this can be overestimated), a great polarization had already begun to take place, and I was being driven over more and more to the liberal position by the extreme racists who were so busily warping facts and condemning me for whatever action I took.

That polarization was reaching a new peak when, early in 1963, John F. Kennedy began to push for a Civil Rights Act that would include a very strong public-accommodations section requiring that any private business involved however remotely in interstate commerce would be forced to open its doors to anyone, black or white. This, of course, was aimed generally at restaurants and hotels across the nation but particularly at those in the South which had managed to close their doors to Negroes by arguing private property rights ("Management reserves the right to refuse admission to anyone"). At this time Atlanta had made enough voluntary progress in desegregating public and private facilities that it was being lauded throughout the rest of the country as a racial oasis in the South—a "City Too Busy to Hate"—and both the city and I, as its mayor, had a generally favorable liberal image; especially when compared to our former rival, Birmingham, which often seemed under the absolute control of rednecks and rabble-rousers. Atlanta *had* made strides during the first three years of the sixties, but the battle line had been drawn quite clearly at the restaurants and the hotels. Everything I had tried in those areas had failed. There had been endless meetings with the hotel and restaurant people over the past three or four years, and no matter what agreement was reached everyone involved would be split in every direction (Maddox must have released statements that he was resigning from the Chamber of Commerce some three dozen times during that period). The issue was mounting rapidly and there seemed to be no solution for it that would please all sides. The hotel and restaurant associations would not even respond to the pragmatic argument that unless they opened their doors to everyone, Atlanta's convention and tourist business—not to mention its favorable national image—would plummet. And the outrage against President Kennedy's proposed public-accommodations section served to further inflame the city, along with the rest of the South and much of the nation. All of the usual conservative voices in the South were using the argument that a public-accommodations bill would be an affront to private enterprise, of course. They were laying the same old stresses that this wasn't a national problem, it should be left up to local governments, which was as if to say the theory that all men are created equal was a local issue. And not only were the usual conservative forces coming out against President Kennedy's bill, they were being joined by most of the liberals. Eugene Patterson of the *Constitution,* the man who had played such a big part in my enlightenment on the race issue, shared the opinion that the bill would be unfair to the private businessman. Governor Carl Sanders, both Georgia senators, and the entire state Congressional delegation—including feisty young Charles Weltner, the liberal Democrat who would later resign from Congress rather than support Maddox when the latter became governor—had come out against the bill. In the beginning, so swamped was I by daily details that I didn't know exactly how I felt about it except that it seemed to *support* the Constitution of the United States rather than to go against it.

It wasn't long before I *had* to stand back and look at the bill and decide whether I was for it or against it. In the spring of that year I received a visit from an old friend, Morris Abram. Only a year earlier, Morris, a debonair young Jewish attorney who had grown up in the south Georgia town of Fitzgerald, had taken on a segregationist lawyer named Buck Murphy in federal court and won the long fight to end Georgia's notorious county-unit voting system. Now Morris was a prominent lawyer in New York, a friend of the Kennedys, and after I had invited him to take a seat in one of the eight Kennedy rockers in the office at City Hall, he came right to the point.

"You're familiar with the public-accommodations bill," he said.

"That's all we hear down here lately."

"The South's pretty upset, I understand."

"Upset?" I said. "I don't know of a single important official in the South who's come out for it. Patterson, Weltner, *no*body."

"That's what I came to see you about."

"What?"

"Ivan, the President wants you to support the bill."

"The Pres—?"

"He wants you to go to Washington and testify."

This stunned me. I was a great admirer of President Kennedy, although we had only met briefly a couple of times. He knew a few things about me through Leonard Reinsch of Cox Broadcasting, which owned WSB in Atlanta, and I could assume he had kept up with what civil-rights progress we had been making and was also aware that I was championing the federal government as the last hope for cities. But for him to send Morris Abram to ask me to go and testify in Washington left me confused. For one thing I was still awed by Washington, even though I had been storming the bastions up there quite a bit lately in search of money for Atlanta. For another, I simply hadn't committed myself yet on the bill I was being asked to support with Senate testimony. And there was something else whirling around in my mind as I tried to come up with an answer.

"Morris, you know the dilemma I'm in on this thing," I said. "I've got a large Negro population down here, and they support me because I've done more for them than anybody else on the political scene in the South. But if I go up there I'm not going to pass the bill or even have a strong influence on it, and if I go I won't stand a chance of getting re-elected in 'sixty-five. It would be suicide for me to go, and you know it." He listened quietly. Being from south Georgia, he certainly *did* know what I meant. I said, "I'll leave it this way. Please tell the President what I said and ask him to weigh it. Discuss it with him personally, Morris, and be sure he fully understands all of the angles. And then if he calls on me and still wants me to do it, if he recognizes that I can't be re-elected and that my testimony isn't going to pass the bill, then I'll go."

It didn't take long for President Kennedy to make up his mind. Soon after Morris Abram's visit a phone call came into City Hall from the White House and a voice said the President was calling. In that clipped, formal Cape Cod accent he was telling me he had made a decision and he wanted me to testify. "You're right," he said, "your testimony alone is not going to pass the bill. But I don't think you are correct in thinking your testimony will defeat you. I think there will be sufficient change in the country by 1965 to where it not only will not defeat you, it will help you get re-elected." I told him I didn't agree with that part but that I felt an obligation to testify if he wanted me to, and that I would go to Washington. So it was settled. I would go.

The testimony was scheduled for July 26 before the Senate Committee on Commerce, giving me little more than two weeks to talk to certain people and prepare my testimony and get myself mentally ready to go. I knew it was not going to be a pleasant trip. I was neither a lawyer nor a man experienced in verbal combat, and I knew I was going into a lion's den. Facing me on the other side of the conference table would be an array of senators who were quite adept at cutting a witness into a million pieces if they wanted to—and I had little doubt that some of those expostulating, bombastic, bigoted Southern conservatives would like nothing more than a chance to have at this mayor of Atlanta in a hearing that was certain to get broad national coverage on television and in the papers.

But as I sat back and took a cold look at the whole situation I gained more confidence in myself and began to feel that the passage of this bill, or something like it, would be the only way all of the barriers of discrimination—not only in the South, but all over the nation—would ever finally be broken down. I looked at what was happening in Atlanta at that very moment. In May the Chamber of Commerce had unanimously approved and then issued a "policy declaration" asking all businesses to desegregate in order to "maintain the city's healthy climate." In response to that, eighteen leading hotels and motels and thirty top restaurants had voluntarily abolished segregation—for conventions only, in the case of the hotels and motels. But that was in downtown Atlanta, and the principal motivation had been one of business pragmatism. What about the others, the thousands of public places in the dozens of small cities and towns on the periphery of Atlanta? Atlanta still would choke to death on its own prejudices if there were only a few scattered hotels or restaurants where a black man could be treated on an equal basis. And what about Macon and Savannah and Columbus and Augusta? What about the small roadside diners and motels on the main North-South route to Florida, in southeast Georgia? I was convinced now that voluntary desegregation of public facilities, worked out on a local level, had gone as far as it was going to go in the South and much of the rest of the United States. The Supreme Court had been very explicit in voiding segregation in 1954, but Congress had sat on its haunches and failed to act. Now Congress was doing the same thing, throwing up smoke-screen constitutional questions about private enterprise that were clearly bellywash to me. It was obvious that the President was going to have to push through a very plain and airtight law that would, once and for all, abolish the practice of segregation. And segregation, as I intended to say in my testimony, was "the stepchild of slavery."

I asked Bill Howland, a former *Time-Life* reporter who was now serving me as an advisor on a part-time basis at City Hall, to help me draft the testimony. We spent long hours together on the testimony, trying to make it as blunt and as explicit as possible. We would talk about Atlanta and how we had made progress up to a point on a voluntary basis, about why Atlanta had been successful while other cities were failing to cope with the problem. Then we went to the heart of it. "Are we going to say that it is all right for the Negro citizen to go into the bank on Main Street to deposit his earnings or borrow money," Bill and I wrote, "then go to the department store to buy what he needs, then go to the supermarket to purchase food for his family . . . but when he comes to the restaurant or the hotel . . . be refused service? I submit that it is not right to allow an American's citizenship to be changed merely as a matter of convenience." The thrust of the testimony would be that the public-accommodations bill should be passed because desegregation would proceed no further without it.

Needless to say, I didn't discuss my intentions to testify with many of my constituents or even my peers in the business community. I knew where they stood. In spite of the recent "policy declaration" by the Chamber of Commerce, I was aware that I would find few, if any, supporters there. In fact, one of the very few in my group that I confided with was Robert Woodruff of Coca-Cola. I took an excerpt of the testimony to his office one day and told him what I was going to do. "You're in a dilemma, and I know it's going to be a very unpopular thing to do," he told me, "but you've made up your mind and you're probably right about it, and I think you should go." He suggested that I modify my testimony to allow for a time delay in smaller towns, which I did. Other than a handful of liberals, Woodruff was about the only white person in Atlanta who told me I should go to Washington and support the bill. Even though the testimony was about finished and I was preparing to leave, I was still agonizing over whether I should go. There were a lot of times when I thought it would be easier to evade the issue after all. If I refused to go, hardly anyone beyond Morris Abram and President Kennedy would ever know the difference. I had no further political ambitions past serving another term as mayor (I *did* want to do that, so I could see to the completion of projects I had begun working on), but there was still the very certain idea in my mind that if I went to Washington and spoke out for the bill I wouldn't have a prayer for re-election.

I was still thinking about backing out at the last minute when my wife, Louise, put everything in a nutshell for me. "If you fail to do what you think is right now," she said, "you will have failed in what was your whole purpose in going into the mayor's office: to do what you thought was right without worry of political repercussions. You'll have a hard time living with yourself the rest of your life if you don't do it. I don't think you can be re-elected if you *do* go, but if you feel it's right, then go and accept the consequences. You'll feel better the rest of your life." I never looked back at my decision after that.

There was one other thing I wanted to do before leaving for Washington. The day before I was to leave I called together the twenty-four top Negro leaders in the city, the people from whom I had learned so much and with whom I shared mutual respect and support. I wanted them to know in advance what I was going to do, so that they wouldn't have to find out about it in the papers or on television, and I met with them on the second floor of the Negro Butler Street YMCA. There was Martin Luther King, Sr., and William Holmes Borders and Rufus Clement and Jesse Hill and A. T. Walden and Benjamin Mays—all of the key Negro leaders who had been at my side during years of crises.

I asked them to sit down, and I told them that I was going to Washington to testify on behalf of the public-accommodations bill and I wanted to read my testimony to them and see what they thought. I felt very good about the testimony, and I very carefully read the 3,500-word statement in the hot upstairs room while a fan droned on and on and the two dozen men quietly and intently listened. When I had read the statement I opened up the meeting for discussion, and they were obviously elated. They knew better than anyone else that no one out of the South had yet testified for the bill. But then there was sort of a straw vote taken, and it turned out that no more than four or five of the twenty-four there wanted me to deliver the testimony. I know Borders and Mays and King, Sr., felt I should go, but the consensus was that they didn't want to sacrifice me for a testimony that wasn't necessarily going to pass the bill. The Atlanta newspapers and big television stations weren't for the bill, the political leaders weren't for the bill, the white man on the street wasn't for the bill, and now even the Negro leaders didn't want me to come out for it. About all I seemed to have going for me was Louise's advice about doing what I thought was right —damn the torpedoes—and I was clinging to that like a starving man with a loaf of bread as I got on the plane alone on the eve of the hearing and flew off to the capital.

The next morning while I was eating breakfast in my hotel room I had a call from Margaret Shannon, Washington correspondent for the *Atlanta Journal* and a lady I have always admired and respected. She had heard I was in the capital to testify, wanted to come up and talk to me about it, and when I explained what I would say and why I would say it she seemed somewhat shocked and perhaps disturbed, a reaction I had gotten used to by now. Shortly after that I went on over to the Capitol, stopping by briefly to visit with Charlie Weltner, and then found the Senate chamber where the hearing was to take place. There was no question that this was going to get a lot of attention. It was one of the larger committee rooms, and although the committee studying the public accommodations bill was small, the room was already filling up with visitors and newsmen and television equipment. The chairman of the committee was Senator John Pastore of Rhode Island, and I had a chance to chat with him for a few minutes before the hearing began. "Senator, I'm always impressed here and a little bit frightened," I told him, and I guess I sounded like a little boy talking to his father. "I'm happy you'd be impressed, Mayor, but I hope you won't be frightened," he said. Sitting in front of a battery of microphones and television cameras, I proceeded to read the testimony I had prepared back in Atlanta. Once I had read the testimony, Senator Pastore said some very kind things about me, noting that is more difficult for a Southerner to do what I was doing than for someone from "where we are reported as being for civil rights"—and ended by saying, "When a man like you comes before this committee today and recites his story in such forthright manner, with such courage, I am proud to be here to listen to you, Sir."

"Thank you, Sir," I said. "I appreciate your kind remarks."

"Senator Thurmond."

They weren't going to fool around. "Mayor Allen, I observe that you are endorsing this so-called public-accommodations bill, is that correct?" Strom Thurmond, the senator from South Carolina, had blood in his eyes.

Strom Thurmond represented the dark side of the South to me. He was the epitome of all the professional segregationists I had ever known—prejudice personified—and a man whom I could not respect in any sense. These men are dangerous only when they are sly and cunning enough to make their prejudices work (George Wallace is like that, but Lester Maddox is not), and Thurmond was smart enough to know what he was doing. As far as I'm concerned, he never really did anything to help the South. He only kept it buried in prejudice and bigotry and hate, kept it so divided, kept it so preoccupied with nigger-nigger-nigger, that the South almost lost its way.

And now here I was, a mere mayor with absolutely no training in law or debate or high-flung oratory, about to be set upon by one of the masters of demagoguery. Thurmond started slowly working me into a trap, by talking in a mock-serious patronizing tone and getting me to repeat much of what I had said in my testimony.

"On separate employment listings, I believe this was voluntary action," he said.

"That is correct."

"Employing firemen, I believe, was voluntary . . ."

"That is correct."

"The handling of real estate, I believe, was voluntary action."

"That is correct."

And then he began to zero in, trying to force me to sound as though I wanted to close down every small restaurant in every small city in Georgia. He wanted to take the fact that much of Atlanta's progress had been voluntary and twist it to prove that all local governments could solve their own problems without the help of the federal government. He wanted to fake me into saying things, such as, if the bill passed, it would be necessary for non-complying restaurants to keep records and addresses of all their customers so that the owners could prove they were not serving interstate travelers. He was trying to blame me personally, in case the bill passed, for closing down businesses in the South. I think the testimony shows I didn't fold, and that this was getting under his skin. "I don't know which comes first, the one business or the two hundred thousand [black] citizens [of Atlanta]," I told him. "I would like to see all of them preserved."

Senator Pastore, as chairman of the committee, soon had enough of Thurmond's questions. He cut in after Thurmond and I had been batting it back and forth for about fifteen minutes, and drew cheers from the packed gallery by reprimanding Thurmond. "I hope that we won't begin to fling at these witnesses the type of 'when did you stop beating your wife?' sort of question, because that, I think, is most unfair," Pastore said. It took a couple of minutes for the lecture to sink in. Thurmond was wanting the floor again, and now the gallery was on him and he was beginning to boil.

"I resent it," Thurmond said.

"Let the Senator from South Carolina resent it," said Pastore, to cheers.

"Mr. Chairman, I am surprised that you permit applauding in this room."

"I didn't do anything about that."

"You did nothing to stop it."

"I can't stop it after it happens."

"Mr. Chairman, if you wish to give vent to the feelings here, and if you wish to have such a common quorum, that is a matter of view while you preside."

"Mr. Thurmond, I don't know who is in this room. It is the general public."

"I can tell you who is in here," shouted Thurmond, who was livid by now. "It is a bunch of left-wingers who favor this bill, and who are taking your position, and you know it."

So it was out now. The exchange between Pastore and Thurmond took another fifteen minutes, and during that time I began to sense the drama of the whole thing. I had gone and given my testimony, and answered a few questions, but I had been the catalyst for something much more than that. This hearing was a showdown between the two ideologies at either end of the civil-rights issue: John

Pastore, the liberal New Englander; and Strom Thurmond, the conservative Southerner. A few more questions were asked of me, one of the other committee members said he felt like the Senate had been "visited by a man of quiet courage this morning," and I was then excused from the hearing. I was headed back to the South, about to find out just how much courage I really did have.

Having been in the middle of it, in the eye of the storm, I didn't realize in the beginning what a stir had been created by the hearing and by my testimony. The next day *The New York Times* published a favorable editorial—"On rare occasions the oratorical fog on Capitol Hill is pierced by a voice resonant with courage and dignity"—as did most other Northern and Eastern newspapers. But over most of the South, where my testimony and the debate between Pastore and Thurmond dominated the papers and television news reports, I found little support. In Georgia, the *Albany Herald* said, "We shake our heads at the Mayor's slick, political moralizing." The *Augusta Chronicle* said I had spoken out for "a bill that would shackle private enterprise with one of the most restrictive burdens ever conceived in our free society." The headline over an editorial in the paper at Rome, which is less than fifty miles from my father's birthplace, read, "Glad Mr. Allen is Atlanta's Mayor." The *Atlanta Constitution* still refused to support the public-accommodations bill but did acknowledge that I had "stood courageously for what he sincerely believed and we admire him for that." Anyway, after the testimony I flew to North Carolina and was met by Louise and some friends for a week end of golf, and that is where I first began to see how deeply the animosity toward the bill and my testimony and myself really ran. I could see my friends that weekend off in the corner by themselves, obviously deeply concerned about what I had done, and all Louise and I could do was try to ignore it and ride out the weekend.

Back in Atlanta the next week, the feedback was reaching its peak. Louise told me she was getting the repercussions, that all over town they were saying I had really blown my stack and that I was through and all of that. There were "indignation meetings" going on all over the place, every night, always with a lawyer present who was playing the same tired games with interpretations of the Constitution. Even some of my relatives got into the act, letting it be known that this was the last insult—that there was no way they could deny what Ivan had done *this* time. Many of the letters and telegrams were vicious: "I wish to nominate you as Mr. Mau Mau of 1963. I understand that you are a half-brother of Martin Luther King"; but because reaction from the Negro and liberal communities was so strongly in support of me, the first week's mail brought 167 favorable letters and 90 against. It was not an easy time for me or for my long-suffering wife. We had to console ourselves with the fact that we had known what I was getting into and there was no sense, and no choice, in looking back at what might have been. I was still certain I had done the right thing, come hell or high water.

Then opinions began to shift. It probably began when the *Constitution* reprinted *The New York Times* editorial. After the passions of the moment had been allowed to simmer, a lot of people (particularly my peers in the business community) began to think, "Well, hell, maybe Ivan *did* do the right thing." Governor Carl Sanders' statement against the bill was printed, and I think those who took the time to go back and compare my stand with his could see whose was more credible and more qualified. Mayor Emeritus Hartsfield went on record as favoring my actions. Dick Rich of Rich's department stores spoke out for me. The hate mail fell off to its usual level of about thirty-five per cent, which may be the percentage of haters we will always have to live with in the South. It wasn't too long after my testimony and the outburst of reaction to it that suddenly I could sense that the image of Atlanta and its mayor was brighter than it had ever been before, and that instead of my testimony being an albatross around my neck it had become, as President Kennedy had so accurately predicted, a medal. My secretaries quickly filled up three or four scrapbooks with the greatest amount of personal commendation *and* condemnation that I would receive during my entire stay in the mayor's office, and those scrapbooks are treasured by me more than any other memorabilia I have from those eight years.

The larger significance of my public-accommodation testimony, however, can't be clipped out and pasted in a scrapbook. It was much more personal than that. I have to be honest with myself and admit that up until the time I had to make the decision whether to go to Washington or not go, my liberalism on the race issue had been based to a large degree on pragmatism: it was simply good business for Atlanta to be an open city, a fair city, a "City Too Busy to Hate," a city trying to raise the level of its poorest citizens and get them off the relief rolls. Although it doesn't seem half so important to me *why* a person is liberal as *whether* he is, and what he does with his liberalism, I am certain that at this point I had finally crossed over and made my commitment on a very personal basis. And I think I took some of my friends with me.

Ivan Allen, Jr.

Two views of the skyline of Atlanta, ten years apart, both taken from the same spot atop the Georgia Baptist Hospital, looking from east to west.

The new Atlanta.

Ivan Allen, Jr., at the site of the Orly crash in Paris, 1962. Edwin L. Sterne, Assistant City Attorney from Atlanta, is at right.

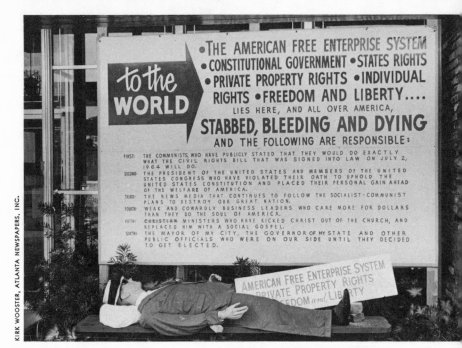

A display in front of Lester Maddox's restaurant, 1964.

Ivan Allen, Jr., and Lester Maddox after the primary election in 1961, before facing each other in the runoff.

*Left,* Maddox standing beside a coffin symbolizing "the death of free enterprise and private property rights" shortly after he closed his Pickrick restaurant rather than serve Negroes.

*Right,* a Klansman pickets in downtown Atlanta during the almost daily racial trouble over desegregating public accommodations, 1964.

*Below,* the first biracial formal dinner in Atlanta, held to honor Martin Luther King, Jr., on being awarded a Nobel Prize. Seated, left to right, Dr. King, Mrs. King, Mayor Allen.

*Top,* Mayor Allen stands atop a police car during the Summerhill riot of 1966; Lt. Morris Redding holding bullhorn, and a SNCC member exhorting the crowd.

*Center,* Mayor Allen trying to reason with Summerhill rioters, September 1966.

*Bottom,* Mayor Allen speaks to the crowd during the riot.

Mayor Allen celebrates in the Braves' clubhouse after they clinched the 1969 Western Division championship of the National League.

Major League baseball comes to the new Atlanta stadium: N. Y. Mets vs. Atlanta Braves during the 1969 National League playoffs.

Mayor Allen escorts Mrs. Martin Luther King, Jr., back from airport, after learning of Dr. King's death, 1968.

The funeral service for Dr. King, Ebenezer Baptist Church. At far right, seated, Mayor Allen leans back to talk to Whitney Young. Standing, from right, are Governor Nelson Rockefeller, Mayor John V. Lindsay and Governor George Romney. Senator and Mrs. Robert F. Kennedy are seated at far left.

Thousands following the mule-drawn coffin of Dr. King through the streets of Atlanta from the church to his burial.

ASSOCIATED PRESS

Mayor Allen holds a daffodil he received from a hippie demonstrator after a sit-in near the Georgia Capitol.

Mayor Allen delivers his farewell address; behind him sits incoming Mayor Sam Massell.

# Part Two

# Re-election

I am not ready to give up Atlanta to those who
say that all cities are sick and cannot recover.
I cannot speak for all American cities, but I
say that Atlanta did not spend the past one
hundred years rebuilding from the ashes to fall
prey now to corrosion, corruption and community discord . . .

—State of the City Address,
January 3, 1966

As my first term neared its end in 1965, it was obvious
that Atlanta was on the move and that the best lay ahead
of us in the second half of the sixties. They were throwing
firebombs into Negro churches and attacking groups of
civil-rights workers in Birmingham and other parts of the
South, but so far we had smoothly desegregated our public facilities and faced the race issue in a pragmatic fash-
ion. The county unit system had been finally buried
forever, and reapportionment had taken place in the state
legislature and in the state's Congressional districts, giv-

129

ing metropolitan Atlanta proper representation in Washington and in the state capitol. In only four years Atlanta had moved from twenty-fifth to twenty-third among the nation's largest metropolitan areas, and was booming like few others. During 1964 we had the nation's second greatest gain in the primary index of growth: new construction. The total value of building permits for the four years since 1962 was $500 million, compared to $400 million for the four-year period before that. The Forward Atlanta campaign's goal had been to add 10,000 new jobs each year (following a year, remember, when the city had actually lost jobs), but we were adding something like 25,000 new jobs a year instead. Unemployment by late '65 had dipped to an incredibly low 2.2 per cent, the lowest in the nation. Department-store sales, an accurate indicator of an area's prosperity, was increasing an average of ten per cent each year, and in 1964 we had the third greatest gain among America's twenty-five largest cities. And the building boom was just reaching its peak. A $22-million improvement program had been completed at Atlanta Airport, which now ranked fourth nationally in passenger enplanements and fifth in commercial operations, and we now had a 10,000-foot parallel runway to keep up with the jet age. The number of hotel and motel rooms had more than doubled, Atlanta Stadium had been dedicated, the new auditorium and convention center was one-fourth finished, twenty-one new buildings, costing at least $1 million each, were on the drawing boards, a Rapid Transit Authority had been set up to study the feasibility of a much-needed rapid-transit system, our urban-renewal program was being called one of the most outstanding in America, Economic Opportunity Atlanta was beginning to gear up in the fight against poverty and illiteracy and crime, and we had even managed to remove the hypocrisy of serving liquor in a "dry" county by passing a mixed-drink referendum. It was clear that Atlanta was on the upswing in almost every area, that she had momentum, and that our efforts in the first half of the decade should start paying off in the second half.

My original plan, when I ran for mayor in 1961, was to carry my Six-Point Program into City Hall and try to make it work and then step down after four years in office. At no time did I have any further political ambitions. My idea was to help make the transition from the Harts- field era a smooth one and then, if possible, pass the job on to some other younger member of the Atlanta business community.

But the position of mayor can grow on you. As the years began to run by, I found out how difficult it is to imple- ment a program in government in a hurry and then to see it through to fruition. I had stumbled through my first year and learned my lessons the hard way—the failing bond issue, the Peyton Road blunder, etc.—had finally gained control of the city's political processes the second year, had gained some national notice as a civil-rights spokesman in the third year, and now could see all of our well-laid building plans beginning to fall in place. What President Kennedy had told me about my going to Wash- ington to testify in behalf of public accommodations— that it would "not defeat you, it will help you get re- elected"—appeared to be true. I was riding the crest of a wave of popularity. I had the black citizens of Atlanta on my side because of my Senate testimony. I had the busi- ness leaders on my side because desegregation had been painless and because this great period of prosperity was upon us. I even had the lower- and middle-class whites on the southeast side, normally bitterly opposed to me, now publicly supporting me because the Braves were on their way to Atlanta Stadium and these people's excitement over major-league baseball transcended their hate and fear of the Negro.

In short, my first four years had been successful, but I knew there was unfinished business to be taken care of and I felt I could be easily re-elected, and in 1965 it came time for me to decide whether I wanted to remain in City Hall for another term. Early that year I had long talks with Louise. It was agreed that I had other things to do, although matters at the Ivan Allen Company were being well taken care of, and that the second half of the sixties promised undue stresses and strains to middle-aged mayors of big American cities. We finally agreed to give it one more shot, and no more. I would run this time, but never again. I would quit while I was ahead, or so I hoped.

I really had no race that year. My only opposition was Muggsy Smith, the insurance man who had cut into my Negro vote during the '61 primary but had finished fourth with only 14 per cent of the vote, and this time Smith found himself without any issues except the Hate-Ivan-Allen issue. He had very little support, and I think the people who voted against me wouldn't have voted for Muggsy Smith under any normal conditions if there had been almost any other candidate. He tried to attack me on the stadium-Braves issue: that I had spent $600,000 for a hurry-up construction job, and then the Braves hadn't come. But we had done a good selling job on the public and made them realize that getting the stadium built in less than one year had, in the long run, saved us from spiraling construction costs; and, of course, the Braves *were* coming for the 1966 National League season. And Smith could hardly attack me on the race issue in an attempt to secure Negro votes, because I had my ace in the hole there.

What a joy it was to go to a Negro rally that year. Before I left for it, I would reach up on a shelf and pull down a green leather-bound book entitled TESTIMONY BY IVAN ALLEN, JR., CIVIL RIGHTS, PUBLIC AC-COMMODATIONS, 88TH CONGRESS. The Negro people are particularly responsive to a certain flair or a dramatic approach, but they also like a certain dignity in their churches and their community houses. So when I would walk into a Negro church with this leather-bound volume it was as though I was carrying a Bible under my arm. They knew I would pull that out in a very formal way and say that I hadn't come to speak to them in terms of what I *might* do or what somebody else might do, or to make some vague political promises. I would simply pull out my civil-rights testimony and read from it about what I *had* done. There aren't many people in political life who can just walk in and completely dominate an audience as I was able to do with Negro audiences during that campaign. This wasn't a newspaper clipping or something taken out of context from an obscure editorial or speech; this was the actual transcript, in a handsome leather-bound volume, holding exactly what I had said in the halls of Congress about the rights of black people and the need to pass tough laws finally granting those rights after centuries of slavery. To say that my reading from the testimony was regarded with great reverence at Negro rallies would be an understatement.

Consequently, I didn't have to worry much about Muggsy Smith's campaign against me. I was able to concentrate on helping to assure the election of those aldermen who had been my friends and supporters during the first term. Every one of the aldermen to whom I gave my endorsement and support were elected, although one or two of them had gone into their campaigns in serious trouble. When it was over, I won without a runoff— 53,233 votes to Smith's 21,907—and I was in a heady, optimistic mood on the night of January 3, 1966, when I

went before the board of aldermen at City Hall—fourteen
weeks before the Braves were to open their first National
League season in Atlanta—to deliver the annual State of
the City Address:

The potential and the promise of election year 1961 have
come full circle. In that year, we who gather here today to survey the past and to consider the future have successfully sought
the high offices which administer the municipal government of
the City of Atlanta. The progress of Atlanta during these four
years has outstripped even the maximum potential we then believed possible, and the performance of this city in all things
significant has far surpassed even the most lavish of promises.
I say to you, gentlemen, unequivocally and with deep humil-
ity, that no group of public officials ever had a finer opportunity to provide leadership than we who were chosen to guide
our city during the period of her greatest growth.

Projected against a background of national economic expansion—with an upward surge in the gross national product
from under $519 billion in 1961 to almost $700 billion in 1965,
with a decrease in unemployment from 4,806,000 in 1961 to
2,966,000 in 1965, and strengthened by confidence in outstanding national leadership—the time was most certainly ripe for
Atlanta to emerge from a static position of just another American city and move vigorously forward as a regional and national
giant . . .

With even the most conservative economists now predicting
that 1966 will produce record highs in almost every growth factor, and with Atlanta already enjoying an enviable position
among American cities, you need not be experts to prophesy
tremendous potential for the years ahead. We are big, with
every promise of growing bigger. And there are those who say
that this very bigness carries in it the seeds of civic self-de-
struction through indifference, through inadequate city services, through growing poverty for some—contrasted with
greater prosperity for most—and through poverty's by-products
of crime and decay. But I am not ready to give up Atlanta to

those who say that all cities are sick and cannot recover. I cannot speak for all American cities, but I say that Atlanta did not spend the past hundred years rebuilding from the ashes to fall prey now to corrosion, corruption and community discord . . . We have the means, the moral determination and the motivation to become, perhaps, not America's largest city—we can wait awhile on that—but her finest city . . . Perhaps we will set a pattern for other cities to follow and thereby create a better way of life for the more than one hundred and thirty million Americans who have cast their lot with the cities . . . This is indeed a time for decision for our beloved city, and I am confident that her five hundred and four thousand citizens will move in behind this bold effort to make Atlanta truly America's finest city within your lifetime and mine . . .

As I pointed out in the address, in the second half of the sixties Atlanta was going to have to cope with an entirely new set of problems—problems that had resulted from our growing from a sedate regional center to a booming national city. Quoting from Lord Chesterfield— "Knowledge may give weight, but accomplishments give lustre, and many more people *see* than weigh"—I said that our accomplishments "have a brilliant lustre" but were "weighted with vital and ever-growing knowledge of our city, its people and its problems."

Atlanta, compared with nine other cities of comparable size, ranked seventh in amount of property tax per capita, eighth in total general revenue per capita, and last in amount of financial aid from the state. We had to come up with more ways to find money to finance rapid transit and urban renewal and pollution-control projects. Although Carl Sanders had done more for Georgia cities than any governor of Georgia had in recent years, we knew now that we couldn't rely on state aid and that the only answer was Washington. I asked for, and got, the creation of the position of Director of Governmental Liaison, which in essence called for a man to run back and forth between Atlanta and Washington carrying a bag to hold federal funds. Money was going to be a problem, and so was what I called "human resources." Now we were well into the era of such federal programs as Head Start and Job Corps, programs of the Kennedy and Johnson administrations that were bold attempts at raising the poor up by their bootstraps and making wage earners of them. Now we were entering a more sophisticated time in history when we were studying and attacking such problems as juvenile delinquency, illiteracy, penal reform, pollution, slum clearance, annexation of suburbs, and grading "postage-stamp parks" in the downtown area. Atlanta's population was growing by 33,000 a year now, and if we were unable to keep up with their needs we would have created a monster rather than a viable city.

There was another major problem on top of us, too, and this wasn't a new one. It was keyed to an old nemesis, the race issue. Tremendous strides had been made during the first part of the sixties in the area of civil rights, but now I was beginning to see the polarization that inevitably had to spring from those strides. The theory of rising expectations had turned out to be true in the Negro community—"Give 'em an inch, they'll take a mile" is how the white racists had always unkindly put it—and now many of the level-headed older black leaders of Atlanta were having difficulty being heard over the calls to revolution of young militants such as Stokely Carmichael and Rap Brown. And every time one of these young blacks talked about burning America down and starting all over again, those whites who had reluctantly gone along with desegregation of the downtown stores and lunch counters fled back to the white supremacist tenets of Eugene Talmadge and Strom Thurmond. A terrible polarization was taking place, and what we needed was cool thinking and level heads. I think I had personally set that sort of pattern for city government in Atlanta and had the support of the responsible black and white civic and spiritual leaders, and Carl Sanders' moderate administration at the capitol was a soothing reality, but we knew that these level heads could be offset by one ultraconservative if he maneuvered himself into the right position. Then, just when we needed him the least, Lester Maddox became governor of Georgia.

Both Maddox and I were native Atlantans who had been raised on the north side of town, attended the city's public schools, operated small sidewalk soda pop stands as kids, and gone on to become the heads of prospering local business firms. But there the similarity ended. I had been graduated *cum laude* from Georgia Tech, but Maddox had dropped out of school in the tenth grade. I had been president of the Chamber of Commerce, but Maddox had huffily resigned from the Chamber dozens of times over the racial issue. I was Presbyterian, he a Bible-quoting fundamentalist. I was a close personal friend of the top Negro leaders in the city, but he had closed down his restaurant rather than serve Negroes. My business was office equipment, his was fried chicken. I was interested in seeing Atlanta grow, but he was primarily interested in seeing Atlanta segregated. We may have been from the same side of the same city, but I can't imagine two public figures being farther apart.

Maddox, as a political figure, had sprung up like a weed when the Supreme Court began making its desegregation decisions in the mid-fifties. He had absolutely no formal training, but he began making a name for himself by firing off inflammatory statements about everything from the Little Rock school situation to the admission of Red China to the United Nations. If it had not been for the race issue we probably would have never heard of Lester Maddox, because he had no administrative capabilities. But he *did* have the race issue in the fifties and sixties, and at a time when cool heads and pragmatic decisions were needed he was busily inflaming an already heated situation by ranting and raving about Communists and left-wingers and race-mixers—all of it mixed, curiously, with quotations from the Bible and righteous talk about how he didn't hate the Negro. The more he was criticized by the Atlanta newspapers, the more he became a martyr, and eventually he took to running a paid two-column ad in the papers each week—"Pickrick Says"—in which he would mix blasts at public officials and the Supreme Court with advertisements for his Pickrick Restaurant. Although many Atlantans sympathetic toward his segregationist ways were embarrassed by his erratic actions ("God bless Lester, he means well," said segregationist comic Brother Dave Gardner during his night-club routine), it was obvious that there would always be a certain strong minority of blue-collar whites willing to vote for him no matter what he ran for. After he had been defeated for mayor by Hartsfield in 1957 and by me in 1961, he ran for lieutenant governor in '62 against Peter Zack Geer, a suave, handsome, golden-throated segregationist, and lost only after forcing Geer to a runoff. Then came Maddox's greatest moment to date, in 1964 when he became a national figure by brandishing a pistol and ax handles at Negroes attempting to integrate the Pickrick and then by closing the restaurant rather than allow Negroes to eat there.

All of this led up to Maddox's announcement in 1966 that he intended to run for governor to succeed Carl Sanders, a handsome young moderate Democrat who had been most cooperative with the city during his four years in office. Ellis Arnall was trying to make a comeback that year, and naturally my support was going to him. I wasn't worried about the prospect of Lester Maddox's winning the race, nor were many others in Georgia at that early date. But as the campaigning continued and we came closer to the primary, it became more and more obvious that we had been underestimating the populist underground appeal of Maddox to that large segment of lower- and middle-class working whites who had been polarized during the civil-rights struggle. All of the groups who usually determine who wins an election—the press, the "power structure," the moderates and liberals, the moneyed interests and the blacks—were arrayed against Maddox, but inexorably he moved forward. With little campaign money, he rode around the state in his own car and got out to nail MADDOX COUNTRY posters on telephone poles and trees. He raved on and on about how the people against him were Communists, about how he could stop "this un-Godly race-mixing," about his friendship with George Wallace, about his background as a "simple working man," about how "nobody wants me but the people." He didn't seem like a serious threat, and the very thought of his candidacy was enough to make the progressives, moderates, and liberals in the state break down with laughter—until that September morning in 1966 when Georgia awoke and found that Lester Maddox (thanks to a substantial cross-party vote from Republicans who thought he would be easier to defeat in a runoff than the other Democratic candidates) had gotten enough votes to win the runoff between him and Ellis Arnall. I immediately came out that morning with one of the strongest statements of my eight years in office:

It is deplorable that the combined forces of ignorance, prejudice, reactionism and the duplicity of many Republican voters have thrust upon the State of Georgia Lester Maddox, a totally unqualified individual, as the Democratic nominee for governor. The seal of the great state of Georgia lies tarnished. The wisdom, justice and moderation espoused by our founding fathers must not be surrendered to the rabble of prejudice, extremism, buffoonery and incompetency.

The usual hate mail came to me after that, of course, but what surprised me was the reaction of most other Democrats in the state. Both U.S. senators, Herman Talmadge and Richard Russell, said they were honor-bound to support their party's nominees and would do so. That was the general feeling with the Democratic party, although young Charles Weltner soon after that resigned from Congress rather than be forced by his party oath to support Maddox. Naturally, Mississippi's Ross Barnett and Paul Johnson were pleased. And George Wallace said, "I think we are reaching the turning point in our struggle against federal tyranny and we are well on our way to destroying it." The election that followed pitted Maddox against Howard ("Bo") Callaway, a wealthy conservative from southwest Georgia. Callaway had a slight edge in the total vote, but election of the governor was handed to the Georgia legislature and they voted along party lines, giving the job to Lester Maddox overwhelmingly.

So now we had another confirmed segregationist in the Capitol in Atlanta, where the Confederate cannons on the front lawn point symbolically in the direction of City Hall across the street, and city leaders feared the worst. Relations between Atlanta and the rest of the state had never been especially good, particularly during the days of the county-unit election system. (Eugene Talmadge used to say he didn't want the vote of anybody who lived where there were streetcar tracks, and the sad fact is that he didn't *need* those votes.) Although Maddox was an At-

lantan in fact, he was not an Atlantan in spirit. His heart
was in the small Southern Baptist churches out in the flat
stretches of segregated south Georgia rather than in the
board rooms of Atlanta corporations. I was apprehensive
over whether we would get any assistance at all from the
new governor—sufficient money for all of the things we
needed like highways and low-income housing and mass
transportation—and whether his election signaled the re-
birth of the hate-Atlanta era in Georgia.

I must admit that my worst fears were unfounded.
Maddox seemed to believe somebody was laying for him
around every corner—poisoning his water, putting needles
in his eggs—and over the next four years he was to put together an astounding record of outlandish actions bordering on vaudeville: riding a bicycle backwards at the new
governor's mansion, passing out Pickrick Drumsticks (autographed ax handles) at the House dining room in Washington, preaching in small fundamentalist churches on
Sunday mornings, holding an open house called "Little
People's Day" at this office, and threatening to run his
wife for governor if the rules weren't changed so he could
succeed himself. He gave Georgia a bad image during his
four years in office, but in reality he neither helped the
state nor hurt it, and the same was true for Atlanta. The
fact that he was ill-educated and totally unprepared for
the job of governor turned out to be a blessing. He simply
didn't know how to function. He wanted so badly to be
a George Wallace or a Strom Thurmond or a Ross Barnett,
but he wasn't equipped to pull it off. He wanted to hurt
Atlanta and its mayor and the liberals and the blacks, but
he didn't know how. In effect, the state was run by the
legislature, which was gaining more muscle than it had
ever had just as Maddox took over—and Lester was free
to spend much of his time spinning his wheels, making
wild statements, and looking over his shoulder.

He was one of the poorest losers I have ever known. When I defeated him in the mayoralty race of 1961 he turned out to be vindictive, never agreeing to cooperate in trying to move the city forward, tucking his tail between his legs and running off to keep up a constant attack against everything we accomplished, leaving little hope that we would ever be able to work together in the future. But when he was elected governor I had no choice but to try to maintain a degree of decorum and attempt to work with him, and I will say that to some extent he adopted the same attitude. Of course time and time again his inconsistency caused problems, and the best example is an incident that took place in the spring of 1969.

The legislature was in session, and one day while I was discussing a possible tax increase with the Georgia Municipal Association in a meeting at the Marriott Motor Hotel I was advised by my office that the governor wanted to see me. I assumed he wanted to talk about the tax increase (I wasn't going to support it unless some of the additional revenue was promised Atlanta), and since there seemed to be no urgency about his call I said I would return it as soon as I could break away from the meeting. In a few minutes my office called again and said the governor needed to see me immediately, that it was a crisis, and I knew it wasn't taxes that had Maddox trembling this time. I asked Captain Morris Redding, my new aide, to pick me up and drive me to the Capitol.

En route, Redding told me what he knew about Maddox's problem. At this time the militant Students for a Democratic Society was taking hold at the University of Georgia in Athens and Georgia State University in Atlanta, and with the legislature in session the local chapter of SDS had decided to march on the Capitol to protest something or other. Apparently, rumors had started getting through to Maddox that the students were going to kill him or burn the Capitol or whatever, because when Redding and I drove up to the Capitol we saw less than a hundred students sitting in the middle of the street while seventy-five to a hundred state highway patrolmen in full battle regalia stood between them and the Capitol. Although I had been through countless demonstrations over the previous ten years and had some knowledge of how to cope with them, it was Maddox's first one, and he was jumping out of his skin. I went on into the governor's office, and Maddox lit into me immediately.

"What are you going to do about that, Mayor?" he said.

"About what, Governor?"

"That mob out there."

"Mob? I saw some students, but—"

"They're out there blocking traffic," he screamed, his face already reddening. "The next thing they'll do is try to break into my office."

"Governor, I don't know what you're talking about."

"Well just look, then. Just look out there."

I looked out the window and all I could see was the state troopers, fitted out in crash helmets and billy clubs and every type of gun in their arsenal. I had never seen such an imbalance of power in all my life. Maddox had panicked and rushed the troopers outside and created a confrontation, and now he wanted to know what *I* was going to do about it. I told him I would go back to City Hall and look into the situation.

When I reached my office I talked to Chief Jenkins and Superintendent George Royal and Captain Redding and some others. In a few minutes I was back at Maddox's office. I told him I would go outside and ask the troopers to move aside, and ask the students to march on the sidewalk if they wanted to march. If they didn't want to do that, I would ask them to go across the street and sit on the lawn at City Hall and I would hear their grievances.

And if they weren't willing to accept either of those two proposals, I said, I would tell the troopers to remove the students by force.

"But no billy clubs," I said.

Maddox blew his stack. "No clubs? I'm not going to have my men subjected to a bunch of anarchists without some protection."

"Anarchists? Governor, I'm perfectly willing to go out there myself. I'm not afraid of a group of kids. They're not going to stick knives in me. They're college students who are demonstrating, and they're entitled to demonstrate. And I'm not going to take a bunch of people out there with billy clubs in their hands." I paused. "Governor, you *have* heard of ax handles, haven't you?"

With that, Maddox flushed a little and finally agreed to my plan. I walked out of his office and down the steps, and after a lot of jawing I got the troopers out of the way, and within minutes the crowd of students had dispersed, and Maddox's crisis of the day was over.

# Years of Growth

Nowhere in the nation can [these] years of phenomenal growth and prosperity in the United States be measured in more glowing terms than in this metropolis of the Old South . . . Businessmen, bankers, politicians and civic leaders all talk about one subject—a national city . . .

—*The Cleveland Plain Dealer*

There is no adequate word to describe Atlanta's physical and economic growth during the sixties. You could use "tremendous" or "fantastic" or "incredible," and you would be correct, but you would still be understating the situation. In that short span of ten years Atlanta grew as much as it had in *all* of its previous history, moving from being a somewhat sluggish regional distribution center to a position as one of the dozen or so truly "national cities" in the United States. In 1959 we were known for Coca-Cola, Georgia Tech, dogwoods, the Atlanta Crackers, and easy Southern living; by 1969 we were known for gleaming skyscrapers, expressways, the Atlanta Braves, and—the price you have to pay—traffic jams. Although by 1969 the metropolitan area ranked only twenty-first nationally—up from twenty-fifth, increasing by 31.4 per cent to 1.3 million —we ranked in the top *ten* in most important growth categories over the 10-year period: downtown construction, bank clearings, air traffic, employment, mercantile construction, *et al.* Atlanta's growth was evidenced everywhere. Eleven of the city's twelve tallest buildings were constructed during the sixties. Atlanta Airport went from the tenth-busiest in the nation to the third-busiest, right behind Chicago's O'Hare and Los Angeles' International. Even the number of telephones increased almost 150 per cent, making metro Atlanta the largest toll-free dialing area in the world. Hotel and motel space nearly tripled, bank clearings doubled, unemployment plummeted at one point to an unheard-of 1.9 per cent. One national magazine labeled Atlanta as "the fastest growing city in the U.S.," and we believed it when we made a survey of what had happened during the decade:

CONSTRUCTION. This is where our growth was most obvious. We ranked eighth in the nation in downtown construction: seventeen buildings at least fifteen floors each (including the forty-one-story First National Bank Building and three others over thirty stories high), the 800-room Regency Hyatt House hotel, and the $100 million Peachtree Center complex connected by aerial walkways. Nineteen office parks were built or announced in the outlying areas (Atlanta being one of the pioneers of that concept)—and a 3,000-acre industrial park became the second largest in the country. In addition, we added 235 warehouses, 167 manufacturing plants, 48 retail department stores, thirteen high-rise apartment buildings, twelve hospitals, and fifty motels-hotels (totaling nearly

10,000 rooms). And about four of every ten private housing units existing in 1969 were built during the decade.

INDUSTRY. Of the nation's five hundred largest industrial corporations, 413 had operations in Atlanta. And more than 170 Atlanta-headquartered firms had operations elsewhere, some on an international scale. We weren't just a regional center any more.

EMPLOYMENT. Atlanta was third nationally in the number of new nonagricultural jobs gained in the sixties, sixth in manufacturing employment. More than 22,000 new jobs were created each year.

SPORTS, CULTURE, ENTERTAINMENT. Atlanta became major league in baseball, football, basketball and soccer during the sixties. The $18 million Atlanta Stadium was the key. Atlanta International Raceway began hosting two major stock-car races per year, and the Atlanta Classic became an annual stop on the professional golf tour. Some $4.5 million was spent on the Atlanta Zoo. Six Flags over Georgia, a privately developed amusement park, was built on 276 acres west of the city. A $5 million restoration was begun on Underground Atlanta, the original main business section of the city. The $13 million Memorial Arts Center and the $10 million Atlanta Civic Center were built. Convention business doubled as a result of this between 1965 and 1969, with 400,000 delegates spending $60 million.

We had hang-ups, of course. We never did manage to get beyond the earliest planning stages as far as a rapid-transit system was concerned, and transportation within the city of Atlanta became more clogged as the days went by. We did not entirely evade the racial unrest plaguing all cities in the latter part of the decade, although considering the fact that we had a 47.1 per cent Negro population and were a Southern city we came out better than most. There was a fast flight to the suburbs on the part of many of our upper-class white citizens, and as the city became more crowded there was a marked increase in crime.

But Atlanta was, all things considered, the city of the sixties in America. In an exhilarating period of growth in most cities throughout the nation, Atlanta grew more than any of the others. There are, of course, many reasons why. For one thing Atlanta faced the racial issue realistically while many others (including, by all means, its former rival, Birmingham) tried to act like it wasn't there or else became adamant in its attitude to it. As the sixties came along, Atlanta, too, was not so provincial as most other cities outside the East; we had a goodly number of branch offices in town already, meaning many of the faces you saw up and down Peachtree Street at lunch hour belonged to bright young people who were bringing new blood and fresh ideas in from other parts of the country. And we had always had a geographical edge on the rest of the Southern cities: between mountains and coasts, transportation center, good climate, national resources, abundant recreation facilities. We also had that hard core of business and civic leaders who had the benevolent attitude that whatever was good for Atlanta was good for them. So the potential was there as Atlanta entered the sixties, and I don't believe it is an exaggeration to say that the Forward Atlanta program unleashed it and became the catalyst for the city's sudden surge forward.

Actually, there had been an earlier Forward Atlanta program back in the twenties, and my father had been co-chairman of it. The project was conceived and financed by Atlanta businessmen to counter the threat of the land boom in Florida, with two main objectives: attract new industry by emphasizing Atlanta's position as a centrally located regional distribution center, and spread the word about Atlanta's virtues to the rest of the nation through national advertising. The first Forward Atlanta program has been credited with bringing a new yearly payroll of $30 million to the city from 1926 to 1929.

It was while I was president of the Chamber of Commerce, just before I resigned to run for mayor, that I decided to get another Forward Atlanta project going. It was included in my Six-Point Program for the Chamber. I knew we had a lot to offer in Atlanta, but it was also obvious that we simply weren't getting the word past the city limits; the Chamber was underfinanced and had only a small staff with no long-range selling plans, and most of the business and civic leaders seemed to have the idea that Atlanta would grow automatically. So the Forward Atlanta Program was launched. More than a million and a half dollars were donated by private businesses to get it going. The Chamber staff was reorganized and expanded. Four primary objectives were set: national advertising, public relations, creation of a research and marketing staff to provide data on Atlanta, and a beefed-up development effort. What we were doing was selling our city like a product. For the first four years the staff included a full-time traveling representative who spent half of his time on the road, calling on industrial and business prospects in major American cities, and the other half back home servicing those he had talked into moving their firm or a branch of it to Atlanta. We began sponsoring *Atlanta* magazine, a slick monthly publication that presented the story of Atlanta to business executives all over the country and quickly began winning awards as one of America's finest city magazines. Every month there were appealing ads in journals like *Business Week* and *The New York Times* and *Newsweek*, telling about Atlanta. At the end of the first three-year phase of Forward Atlanta, there was a unanimous vote from the two dozen or so top sponsors that they wanted to continue. When it came time to develop Phase III, the last three years of the sixties, Forward Atlanta's goals showed that we had raised our sights considerably beyond merely trying to attract new industry. Now we were shooting for national headquarters operations and planning to take on the problems the earlier Forward Atlanta programs had brought: traffic congestion, housing, mass public transportation, and pollution. Forward Atlanta was the leading program of its type in America, and during the sixties some 150 cities sent delegations to Atlanta to talk with Chamber of Commerce officials about how they could get the same thing going.

I doubt that any of this growth in Atlanta during the decade would have been possible, however, without the financial assistance we managed to get out of Washington, D.C. Much of our success was owing to the support, financial and otherwise, of the so-called "power structure." And we were able to pass the largest tax increases over an eight-year period that the city had ever had, by adding a sewer service charge to the water bill and by rewriting an outdated business license law and by other means. But where it was reasonably easy to solve the day-to-day financial problems of the city itself, there was a certain point beyond which we could not go without outside help: primarily in the areas of highway construction, urban renewal, and assistance to the poor. I knew better than even to dream that we would get much of a break from the state of Georgia, because that old anti-Atlanta feeling still persisted, and most state politicians still seemed more concerned with building roads in obscure rural counties than helping Atlanta solve its awesome housing and transportation and slum problems. The only place to go for money was Washington.

I had seen what Mayor Richard Lee was doing with federally funded programs in his city, New Haven, Connecticut. Lee was probably the first American mayor to fully realize that basic urban help had to come from the federal government, and he unabashedly went after it. With sound long-range planning and a fantastic amount of Washington money, Lee practically rebuilt New Haven and made it a model city for the rest of the nation to follow. I got to know Dick Lee, inviting him to Atlanta on several occasions and running into him at various meetings of mayors, and decided to follow his example by beating a regular path to Washington.

Atlanta was in a perfect position to obtain huge chunks of federal money. It was, of course, the Southeastern regional headquarters for almost all of the federal agencies, making it possible for us to have direct communications with the regional representatives. Then, too, we had befriended Washington by acting with moderation on the race issue. As nobody wants to do business with someone who doesn't feel kindly toward their projects, I began to champion any federal project that came along: Head Start, Job Corps, urban renewal, Model Cities, all of them. Too often during the sixties a mayor would accept federal money and then start screaming when the people who had given him the money simply wanted to have some control over how the money was spent. But I was the Southern mayor who had gone to testify before the Senate in behalf of the public-accommodations bill. I was the Southern mayor whose city, rather than being too far gone to be saved, had a chance to become a new kind of city if it had planning and responsible leadership *and enough money*. I was the Southern mayor with enough self-confidence about the race issue that I didn't feel it necessary to damn Washington to become re-elected. So I became the champion of the federal government in the

South—their fair-haired boy, so to speak—and it paid off.

I would say that Atlanta and New Haven got more federal money and did more with it, in proportion to their needs, than any other city in the nation during the sixties. In fiscal 1968 alone, the federal programs brought almost $60 million—nearly equal to the total annual operating budget of the city—to Atlanta. Atlanta got one of the first six grants from the Office of Economic Opportunity and was one of the original group in the Model Cities program. During my second term I put an aggressive young former Economic Opportunity Atlanta officer, Dan Sweat, in charge of governmental liaison, and while I was taking every possible opportunity to praise the programs of the federal government, Dan was constantly hounding the regional representatives and occasionally flying to Washington in search of funds. Low-income housing was the first federal program we benefited from. Then came urban renewal, the Interstate Highway system, OEO, and all of the various programs under it, such as Manpower and Head Start, and finally the Model Cities program for renovating slums. For the first time in history, the federal government had found a champion of its cause in the South—Atlanta—and it handsomely and gratefully rewarded us.

The real symbol of the new Atlanta—the single structure that signified our arrival as a national city—was Atlanta Stadium, which was built in an incredible fifty-one weeks during 1964 and 1965 and became the home of the baseball Braves of the National League and the Falcons of the National Football League. Sitting as it did beside a hundred-acre expressway interchange where three major interstate highways connect, its baby-blue seats and gleaming light towers glistening in the sun, the Stadium was visible and literal proof that Atlanta was a big-league city. Certainly, major-league sports became another profitable "industry" for us: by the end of the decade it was bringing in a total of $18 million a year in new money, but the real value of it all was less tangible. All of the growth indexes in the world couldn't do what major-league sports did in awakening the people of Atlanta and the rest of America to the fact that we really were a major-league city now. Atlanta's baseball appetite, for example, had been whetted in the past by the Atlanta Crackers ("Yankees of the Minor Leagues") of the Class AA Southern Association. The opposition had been Little Rock, Birmingham, Mobile, and the other larger Southern towns; and the heroes had been local favorites like Bob Montag, Art Fowler, and Poochie Hartsfield: minor-league sports for a minor-league town. Now, however, the opposition included the San Francisco Giants and the Chicago Cubs and the St. Louis Cardinals, and the heroes were Henry Aaron and Clete Boyer and Rico Carty. This was the final indication to us that we had made it to the top.

Getting the Stadium built, and finding somebody to play in it, was not easy. Sports was suffering a recession in Atlanta as we entered the sixties. Minor-league baseball was dead, for all intents and purposes, and the Crackers were dying with it. We still had Georgia Tech football, of course, but the rest of the sports scene was bleak: Friday night wrestling at the old City Auditorium, stock-car racing, golf, tennis, bowling, boating on the lakes north of the city. One of the original goals of the Forward Atlanta program in 1961 was to build a municipal stadium, but when I went into office I found that it is one thing to propose something of this magnitude and another to get it done. For one thing, the board of aldermen considered it too much of a political risk to be included in a general bond issue. And for another, we were then so preoccupied with the racial issue that it was almost impossible to stir up any interest in an expensive project that involved—after all—only games. There had been some attempts made to create interest in bringing pro football to Atlanta. A colorful entrepreneur named Bill McCane went so far as to build an "erector set" stadium in DeKalb and stage some American Football League exhibitions there, but all of them failed miserably. The only way you were going to lure major-league sports to a city was to have, or to show you could have, an acceptable stadium.

During my first year in office I made a number of attempts to generate interest in building a stadium to house major-league baseball and football and its vast audiences. I had no luck with the aldermen, of course. It was obvious that the voters were still unaware of Atlanta's growth potential, the need to spend money now to make money later, when they voted against the $80 million bond issue. I had even been unable to convince my peers in the business community of exactly what a stadium and major-league sports could mean to the city. I called several luncheon meetings with representatives of the local Touchdown Club that first year, trying to see if I could find some sponsorship for the building of a stadium, but even these men, the most avid sportsmen in town, couldn't seem to understand that Atlanta was no longer a mere regional city. I was taking it upon myself to sell the city on its potential for greatness, and apparently doing a poor job of it. I remember at one of these luncheon meetings having Jesse Outlar, sports editor of the *Constitution,* come up to me and say, "You're asking someone else to do a job that only the mayor of the city can do." Somewhat defensively, I said, "What do you mean by that?" He told me, "There hasn't been a stadium built in this country in recent years that wasn't built by the enthusiasm and leadership of the mayor himself."

It wasn't until the spring of 1963 that we began to make any headway. I had a call one day from the other sports editor in town, Furman Bisher of the *Journal*, telling me he was bringing in a fellow named Charles O. Finley. I've always been a big baseball fan, the kind who starts his day off by reading every line in every box score, and I certainly knew about Charlie Finley. He was the controversial owner of the Kansas City Athletics of the American League, with not too solid a reputation among the staid traditionalists in baseball's hierarchy, and after a poor season at the gate he was threatening to move his club on to greener pastures again. Bisher said Finley was coming to look at possible stadium sites and that he might want to build one and move the Athletics to Atlanta. We had three basic sites in mind at this time, recommended after a survey financed by some of the philanthropic interests in the city, and Bisher said he would take Finley around and show him the sites.

A day or two later, Bisher called again and said Finley wasn't interested in anything he had seen and was ready to go back home. "Can you think of anything else to show him?" he said. I happened to be facing a map on my office wall that outlined the urban-renewal areas in Atlanta, and my eyes fell on a large acreage adjoining the expressway interchange: what we referred to as the Washington-Rawson area, which was being cleared of its decaying slum houses and had no immediate plans for use. "I've got the greatest location in the world," I told Bisher (in pure desperation, since I wasn't sure what we could do with the area and knew little about how much land would be required for a stadium), and George Royal and I went by to get Bisher and Finley so we could show them the area.

I had ridden over Washington-Rawson many times. At one time it had been one of Atlanta's nice neighborhoods,

with plenty of magnolias and beautiful old homes surrounded by stone walls, but it had deteriorated into one
of our worst slums and now was being cleared under the
urban renewal program. We rode to the top of the hill
overlooking the expressways, got out of the car, and
walked among some old magnolias and weeds. I let Finley take his time looking around, trying to picture in his
mind how a stadium might fit in there, and finally said to
him, "Mr. Finley, this is the finest site in America for a
municipal stadium."

"What are those buildings down there?" he said.

"That's Five Points. Downtown Atlanta."

"What's all that construction over there?"

"Where four interstate highways come together."

"How big is the interchange?"

"Thirty-two lanes," I said. "Biggest interchange in the
South."

To say the least, Finley was impressed. He said, "Mr.
Mayor, I agree with you. This is the greatest site for a
stadium that I've ever seen. I tell you what. If you'll build
a stadium here, I'll guarantee you I'll bring the Athletics
here just as soon as it's finished."

We thought we had reached an agreement with Finley,
from the way he was talking. I took him by to talk with
Mills Lane that afternoon, and when he left town
the next day he again said he would bring the Athletics
to Atlanta if we put up a stadium on the Washington-
Rawson site. As soon as he had left, I went by and got
Mills Lane and drove him over to show him the area just
as I had done with Finley. It didn't take Lane thirty
seconds to say, "This is it."

"I don't know how we overlooked it all this time," I said.

"What do you want to do?"

"Build a stadium right here."

"How bad do you want this stadium, Ivan?"

"Bad."

"You've got it," he said. "Tell you what. If you'll re-create the old Stadium Authority and appoint the people I recommend, and make Arthur Montgomery chairman and me treasurer, I'll pledge the full credit of C&S Bank to build it. And if that's not enough to get it done, you and I can't get it done."

When Mills Lane commits himself to something like that, I had learned, you can count on its being accomplished. I finally had found somebody who was going to build Atlanta a stadium, and fortunately it was the one man in town who had the enthusiasm and the resources, plus an understanding of the risks involved, to do it. We were ready to go now. I began carrying out a calculated plan of bringing twenty or twenty-five of our most prominent citizens—press executives, bank presidents, heads of the major companies—to the site, giving them the grand tour as I had Finley and Lane, so I could get them excited over the idea of the stadium. News of what was going on broke in the newspapers. The Stadium Authority started holding meetings. Major-league fever was catching on all over town. When the major-league All-Star Game was played in Cleveland that summer, a large delegation from Atlanta sallied forth in search of a stadium occupant.

We were shot down the minute we got to Cleveland. The American League was having its annual meeting in connection with the All-Star Game, and we were flatly informed by Joe Cronin, the president of the league, that Charlie Finley didn't have enough votes from the other owners to move his club out of Kansas City. The American League would like to have a club in Atlanta some day, he said, but there was nothing available at the moment. The next day, however, we were in business again. Arthur Montgomery had arranged a lunch for us with a group of the Milwaukee Braves' major stockholders, and a remarkable rapport developed between them and our group— almost all of us were fairly young, highly successful businessmen. They said they were unhappy with the attendance and the political leadership where they were, and wanted to leave Milwaukee. They had a contract with the city, but everybody was assuming that could be settled on a financial basis. There were no specific arrangements made during the long luncheon we had that day, but we did begin to talk about the possibility of moving the Braves from Milwaukee to Atlanta. The courtship was on.

Immediately, Mills Lane began his moves. He brought together two architectural firms, gave them a contract and put up the money for them to draw up plans for an ideal stadium. That September I went on an African safari, the only major time I was away from Atlanta during my terms as mayor, and when I returned the first thing I did was drop by the C&S Bank to see Lane. I was, frankly, beginning to get cold feet. We had no specific agreement with the Braves, we had never met with the county commissioners, we had never met with the board of aldermen. There was just Lane and the members of the Stadium Authority, Arthur Montgomery, and myself. Lane showed me the plans that had been drawn while I was gone, and it was then that I realized the size of this project and the speed in which it was moving. "Mills, you have no security on this thing," I said. "You're in awfully deep, and I think it's time you took some steps to protect yourself and the bank." He simply told me, "You go back over to City Hall and run the city's business, and let me run this show."

The plans for the stadium were completed toward the end of the year and sent to the Braves management, which made certain necessary changes, and then in February of 1964 Lane and Bob Richardson and I arranged for a secret meeting in Chicago with their top officials.

This is when we made our agreement that the Braves would come to Atlanta. We couldn't draw up a full contract, which would have been premature, but instead came to a verbal understanding that we would immediately begin work on the stadium, and the Braves would come to Atlanta for the 1965 season. We sealed it with a handshake and went back home to make the announcement and start work on construction of the stadium.

I can't imagine a more ambitious idea than trying to build something of this magnitude in twelve months, which is what we had to do if the stadium were to be ready for the opening game of the 1965-66 National League season. Outside of Grady Hospital, this was the largest construction project that had ever been undertaken in Atlanta. The usual time allotted to something like this would be two or even three years, but we were paying a $600,000 premium to the contractors to finish it in one year. In the long run, though, building it in a hurry was probably the most economical thing to do because we got our money at three per cent interest and started construction before building costs began to escalate. How we ever built something that large without a strike or some other slowdown, I'll never know. But all during the summer of 1964 this magnificent structure was slowly rising out of the ground, like another phoenix from the ashes, and the construction of the stadium—right there at the interchange, for everybody to see—had baseball fever running high in Atlanta. It was the symbol that we had broken away from the old small-town attitudes and were moving up a notch to join the very biggest cities in the United States.

It would take a separate book to relate what happened next (and Furman Bisher wrote it, *Miracle in Atlanta*). We went to New York early in 1965 to sign the final contracts and make it official that the Braves would move to Atlanta in time to open that season there, but we wound up in court with the city of Milwaukee. After half a century in Boston the Braves had moved to Milwaukee in 1953 and had gone over the million mark in attendance five different seasons and the two million mark four times. But for three consecutive years now (1962, '63, and '64) the club had not reached one million, which was the main reason it wanted to move. The city of Milwaukee suddenly cared about their Braves, and the legal hassle that exploded became the top story on sports pages all over the country for several months and wound up costing both cities a considerable amount of money in legal fees (in Atlanta's case, $800,000). It was eventually ruled that the Braves would have to play out their contract in Milwaukee (where they drew only 555,584 fans during the '65 season) before being allowed to transfer to Atlanta. It had cost us a premium of $600,000 to have Atlanta Stadium completed in fifty-one weeks, and now all we had to show for it was one final summer of watching the Atlanta Crackers. That became an issue during my campaign for re-election in late '65 ("Allen's Coffin," some called the stadium), but all was forgotten on the night of April 12, 1966, when 50,671 jammed the place for the regular-season opener for the new Atlanta Braves. I had spent many hours lying awake in the middle of the night, thinking about that empty stadium and how I had led Mills Lane into building it, and being there that night to throw out the first ball for the first Braves game had to be one of the greatest thrills of my life.

Getting a big league professional football team into Atlanta turned out to be an easier proposition, though we had our anxious moments. We felt Atlanta was a plum for either of the two major pro football leagues. There was no big-time pro football in the South, just as there was no major-league baseball until the advent of the

Braves, and yet the South was virtually the cradle of football interest. High school and college football in the South has been a way of life for longer than anybody can remember. And, of course, with the long-drawn-out autumns that we have in Atlanta we could offer the perfect climate to a pro team. Finally, we already had a perfect stadium that could seat about 59,000 fans. A professional team could come to Atlanta and become, in effect, the property of the entire region, drawing from all over the Southeast and raking in tremendous profits from exclusive television rights.

While we were still fighting the city of Milwaukee over the Braves, it occurred to me during the summer of 1965 that we should get busy trying to come up with a pro football team for Atlanta Stadium. I had a passing acquaintance with the commissioners of both leagues (Joe Foss of the American Football League and Pete Rozelle of the National Football League), and late that summer Arthur Montgomery and I went to New York to call on both of them. It was a courtesy call, and we got courtesy answers: well, yes, we'd like very much to add Atlanta to our league; there won't be any expansion until 1968, but you are high on the list when expansion comes. Montgomery and I came back home with long faces. We weren't even assured of getting the Braves at that time, and now we were a long way from getting pro football.

It was time for me to start looking around for help again, but I had just about exhausted my resources. I couldn't ask Mills Lane to extend himself any further, after his involvement in the stadium. I had run Arthur Montgomery's legs off, naming him chairman of the Stadium Authority. Robert Woodruff had let me know some time earlier that he simply couldn't take on major-league sports, at his age and after the support he had given the city in projects like the cultural center. I really didn't know where to turn until I suddenly thought of Leonard Reinsch at Cox Broadcasting, the group that ran WSB radio and television. Leonard, I knew, was one of the best salesmen in the country. He also had, at that very moment, strong business reasons for wanting to see Atlanta secure a pro football franchise. The NBC television network had been beaten to the punch by CBS in the bidding for pro football television rights: CBS won the contract with the NFL, and NBC had to settle for the weaker AFL. It would behoove NBC to put an AFL team into the South, sewing up this vast virgin territory and to some degree offsetting their loss of the NFL television contract. Since WSB was an NBC affiliate, Leonard Reinsch was the logical man for helping me to land an AFL team for Atlanta.

Reinsch and I must have been thinking on the same wavelength, because the day after I started working on this idea I had a visit from Ray Moore and Don Elliott Heald of WSB. They were proposing that Atlanta go after an AFL franchise. "Look," I said, "why don't *you* do it? You've got more leverage than the city of Atlanta does on this thing." They lit up and shot out of my office, and thirty minutes later Leonard Reinsch was calling me. "I'm going to go to work on it," he told me, and when he tells you that he means it. He would call me from Dallas on his way to Denver, and then he'd call from Denver that night as he was leaving for Washington. Then he'd see Foss in New York and come by to give me a report on his way to Oakland. He almost bought the Denver Broncos, almost got the San Diego Chargers, nearly came up with a deal in Philadelphia. But it couldn't be done. The only thing we could do, he finally told me, was get an expansion team. Atlanta could get the franchise if somebody could get to New York Jets owner Sonny Werblin and talk him into supporting Atlanta instead of Philadelphia when it came to a vote. That brought me full circle, back to Robert Woodruff. There were few men Sonny Werblin admired more than Robert Woodruff of Coca-Cola, and if anybody could sway him it would be Woodruff. I went to see him immediately; he said he would call Werblin, and within forty-eight hours the American Football League was meeting and awarding an expansion team to Atlanta.

Leonard Reinsch came plowing back into Atlanta and called me at 11:30 that night. "Ivan, I've got the contract and I'm coming over to your house," he said, like a kid on Christmas. He showed up at midnight with a signed contract from the AFL, turning over a franchise to Atlanta for $7.5 million. That was too much for an AFL franchise, but Reinsch was willing to pay it. "Have you signed up the Stadium Authority?" I asked him. "They've got to come to me," he said. "I've got the franchise and Atlanta's got to have it." What he didn't know was that Pete Rozelle of the NFL had gotten wind of the deal with the AFL, and he was headed for Atlanta himself.

Before we could even get with the Stadium Authority the next morning, Rozelle was already in town looking for somebody to take an NFL expansion team. For several months we had been flying around the country with hat in hand, begging for a pro football team, and now all of a sudden we were being courted by both of the major pro leagues. The city was in a stew. We had about resigned ourselves to waiting two or three years for pro football, but now we could take our pick of which league we wanted. There was really no doubt which one we would take, because at that point the AFL was still the weak sister of the two. If we had taken the AFL franchise we would have been run out of town. So I got a call from a wealthy young insurance man named Rankin Smith, who had been recommended to Rozelle by Carl

Sanders, and when he said, "Do you have any objections to my bringing NFL football here?" I gave him my blessings. Poor Leonard Reinsch had done all of the legwork and had been the catalyst, but had lost out to a man who didn't have to lift a finger to get the franchise. But we now had major-league baseball and football: the Braves opened in Atlanta in April of 1966, the Falcons in September, making us the only city that had ever added big-league football and baseball in such a short span, and soon after that came the Atlanta Chiefs of the North American Soccer League and the Atlanta Hawks (who transferred from Saint Louis) of the National Basketball Association. With the Braves drawing more than one million fans each year, the Falcons selling some 45,000 season ticket books, and the Hawks coming up with Pete Maravich of LSU, the most exciting player in the history of college basketball, Atlanta became the sports center of the Southeast in a remarkably short period of time. By the end of the decade it was estimated that nearly $60 million a year was generated by major-league sports in the Atlanta area. Most important, though, these teams were visible proof—just as Atlanta Stadium was—that Atlanta had arrived as a national city and was truly a major-league city in every way.

Heady as the boom of the sixties might have been in Atlanta, we had to make certain that we kept our guards up against a cancer that has always accompanied rapid expansion in every major American city: organized crime. When you have hotels and restaurants and night clubs sprouting almost as fast as you can grant building permits, when you have major-league sports bringing in thousands of sporting types to your stadium the year around, when you have millions passing through your city each year on business or pleasure, when you have people not native to the city coming in from every corner of the nation and the world (without that very important quality of innate civic pride that comes from staying in your own home-town), it is virtually impossible to keep up with every-thing or everybody in your city. The huge crime syndi-cates (Mafia, Cosa Nostra, the Mob, whatever you want to call them) operate by investing in a legitimate-looking "front" business while most people are looking the other way (most of them out of apathy, some by design), and once that beachhead is established there is no way to stop them from spreading like mushrooms. When one termite gets his foot in the door, the house falls.

Halfway through the decade, however, Atlanta—as far as we and the Justice Department could tell—was the largest American city still reasonably free of Mafia influ-ence. This is not to say that Atlanta's skirts were clean, or that a citizen could walk any street in town at night without looking over his shoulder. During the ten-year period from 1955 to 1964, major crime in Atlanta had in-creased by 142 per cent—fifteen times faster than popula-tion—making our crime rate in almost every category during 1964 substantially higher than it was in other cities of comparable size in the United States. The term "major crime" is applied statistically to categories such as rape, burglary, robbery, larceny, murder, and automobile theft. With the exception of auto theft, the crimes in which the syndicates usually interest themselves (gambling, illegal liquor, prostitution, drugs, *et al*) are classified as "minor." We were doing badly there, too, even if the strings *weren't* being pulled from New York and Miami. A grand jury estimated that illegal gambling in the Atlanta area *before* the arrival of the Braves, Falcons, Hawks, and Chiefs came to $18 million a year ($80,000 was bet on one local high-school football game). Atlanta was still the "moonshine capital of the world," marketplace for ninety per cent of the 50,000 gallons of moonshine produced each week in the ragged hills of north Georgia (where it was estimated in 1965 that on any given day there were at least 650 moonshine stills going full blast). The city's auto-theft rate was three-and-a-half times the national average, 4,210 stolen cars in '64 totaling about $3 million in losses. Those were the three biggest categories where syndicated crime could easily move in, and behind them were several others: lottery (one of the twelve known large lottery or "bug" operations was broken up in 1965, and found to be doing a $2,000-a-day business, though the usual wager was for less than one dollar), prostitution (fifteen hotels, the Atlanta Commission on Crime and Juvenile Delinquency learned, were considered excellent "hustling" places by the prostitutes working the city), and narcotics (indictments by the Fulton County Grand Jury increased from thirty in 1964 to eighty the next year, and it went out of sight two years later when the city gained a sizable hippie community).

But there was still every indication that what organized crime there was in Atlanta was controlled locally, by what was being dubbed the "Dixie Mafia," rather than by the intricate worldwide syndicates. Generally speaking, the men who were in charge of Atlanta's loosely constructed crime operation were "good ol' boys" who had grown up in the city's white slums or in the small dusty towns out in the Georgia hinterlands. They had started at the bottom by running moonshine out of the mountains or pimping for a bewildered country girl in a walk-up flat or running card games in the rear of garages or boosting hubcaps and selling them to used auto-part dealers. The ones who were smart enough or aggressive enough had gone on to bigger things—moonshine distributors in certain sections of the city, bosses of organized auto-theft rings, lottery kings, bookmakers—but no matter how big they got or how much money they took in they remained semiliterate hayseeds whose survival instinct far surpassed their organizational genius. Once a good ol' boy, always a good ol' boy. It seemed to me that the cultural gap existing between these Bible Belt thieves and the Mafiosi was so wide that it was hardly possible that the two groups could even be civil to each other, much less join forces to become partners in crime. It was utterly beyond my imagination that a fast-talking Sicilian hood in a white-on-white tie and $100 alligator shoes and a shiny black suit could blow in from New York or Miami and hope to get so much as the time of day from one of "our" boys. The Mafia was tightly organized into "families," thought in terms of billions of dollars, operated all over the world, systematically murdered anybody getting out of line, and were first- or second-generation Americans. The organized crime leaders in Atlanta, on the other hand, were concerned only with their respective corner of the block, thought in terms of nickel-and-dime lottery tickets or $5 jugs of homemade whiskey and were leery of anybody who was not a white Anglo-Saxon Protestant Georgian. To worm its way into a city, the Mafia needs three basic things: public apathy, protection from high officials inside the city government, and some contact with the local machine. We felt we were in good shape on all three counts as we reached the halfway point in the decade. That civic pride which had been the catalyst for the tremendous growth of recent years was an assurance that Atlanta's citizens would care a hell of a lot if big-time crime moved in. There had not been a scandal in City Hall for thirty-odd years, and I had complete faith that the key men in all departments of our city government, particularly Police Chief Herbert Jenkins and his superintendents, wouldn't break the streak. Then, too, we had a sort of fifth column in that the good ol' boys might help us, however unconsciously, by keeping the doors shut.

Atlanta was rapidly beginning to change, though, sprawling in every direction, losing the distinctive Southern charm it had always been known for, becoming more cosmopolitan, getting busy and fat and dirty and noisy. By now, it had become a national city, but just as I was standing before the board of aldermen on the third night of January, 1966, the re-elected mayor giving his glowing State of the City address, thunderclouds were developing. The Commission on Crime and Juvenile Delinquency was about to release its weighty report. "There is no question but that Atlanta is like a ripened peach ready to be picked by national syndicates, when they decide to make a concerted effort to move in on organized criminal activities here," the report said. "The same factors which make Atlanta's economy flourish make our city extremely attractive to organized crime elements." The signs that the Mafia was beginning to look our way came soon enough. They were small signs and could have been judged as insignificant if they had not kept coming, slowly but inexorably. The body of Detroit syndicate "hit man" Robert Dunaway was found in the trunk of a car parked at Atlanta Airport, obviously the victim of a Mafia assassination. When Mafia associate Tommy Gambadero was arrested and convicted for using fraudulent credit cards, his $50,000 bail was arranged by Carmine Persico, Jr., of the Joe Colombo family in New York. In December of 1967 investigators found a little black book in the Atlanta apartment of Olga Daniels, a former madam, with the names of three Mafia associates and the date November 10, 1967, circled—that was the day the three were machine-gunned to death in a Queens, New York, restaurant. And all along there was an increase in the number of

Mafia advance men known to be coming into the city, trying to tie in with local hoods or set up legitimate "front" businesses. By 1967 we were keeping a close watch on our flanks, wondering how long we would be able to boast of being the only major city in America free of Mafia influence.

In the summer of that year I had a call one day from Jack Tarver, the president of Atlanta Newspapers, who asked me if I had heard anything about a big real-estate transaction involving the Bel Air Hotel out on Peachtree Road. The Bel Air was at one time an elegant little place, formerly known as the Colonial Terrace Hotel, but it wasn't paying its way with its few residents and even fewer tourists. Tarver told me a couple of men from Miami had paid $1.1 million for the hotel and the grounds, and that they had announced plans to remodel and open as the Atlanta Racquet Club. That was the first I had heard about it, even though it *was* a large transaction. A mayor just cannot keep up with the thousands of real-estate deals that go on in a big city, nor does he usually try. But as the summer continued, and we moved into fall of '67 I began to hear a lot of talk about the proposed new club. Workmen were already swarming over the building and grounds, remodeling the interior and exterior, grading for a number of elaborate tennis courts and installing lounges and dining rooms. Several prominent Atlantans had agreed to serve on the board of directors, and there was a good deal of excitement within the young swinging set in town that this was going to be a wonderful, exclusive in-town tennis club on the order of the Palm Bay Club in Miami. A large preopening party was held late in the fall (Louise and I were invited, but couldn't make it), and I heard it was a swinging bash attended by many of

Atlanta's bright singles and young marrieds, in addition to the press and the board of directors. When I was asked to cut the ribbon to mark the formal opening of the club, I agreed.

In the meantime, however, the two principal new owners applied for a liquor license. The application requires fingerprinting, and their fingerprints were routinely forwarded to the FBI central file. The FBI report on these two men was sent to the Atlanta Police Department on the very day before I was to go out for the ribbon-cutting at the Racquet Club, and when it was called to my attention I was stunned. The men were also partners in a string of seafood restaurants in Miami, Fort Lauderdale, and Key West. One, born in Lawrence, Massachusetts, had been in the hotel and restaurant business for many years, and his record showed only two arrests and convictions—for operating a gambling house and for a minor liquor violation—both in the early fifties. The other, born in Hackensack, New Jersey, had been convicted over a twenty-five-year period for stealing a car, tearing up a public telephone booth, and beating his ex-wife's suitor. But the part of the report that frightened us was the FBI's recounting of some vague associations with known Mafia figures. For instance one of them, the report said, was close to Charles Tourine—had let him use his apartment in New York, had gotten him a Cadillac, and had "accidentally" bumped into him one time in Italy. I wasn't quite sure what to do when presented with this information. On the record both of these men might have been respectable enough, but off the record they appeared to have connections with the wrong kind of people. Maybe this, I thought, is the way the Mob plans to get its foot inside Atlanta: with an exclusive, respectable-looking jet-set tennis club. I didn't want to be unfair to these two outsiders by overacting, but the only thing worse than that would be to underreact.

The first thing I did was call the city attorney and ask him if the city and I personally would be free from libel if I furnished the information in the FBI report to the prominent Atlanta citizens already listed on the board of directors of the Racquet Club, who apparently suspected nothing. Henry Bowden said I was all right as long as I quoted from the FBI file, and that he thought I should do it. Next I called Jack Tarver, who checked out the two men through his sources in Miami and reported back to me that their reputation there was not good, and he thought the FBI report sustained that position. Finally I called in three of the Racquet Club board members I knew well (one of them was Jim Townsend, founding editor of the Chamber of Commerce's *Atlanta* magazine, who was in public relations now and was handling the Racquet Club account), and read the report and told them to take whatever they thought was the appropriate action. They resigned that afternoon, just as I was advising the Racquet Club that the mayor wouldn't be there for the ribbon-cutting.

The next day one of the prominent lawyers in Atlanta invited me to lunch at the Commerce Club. While we were eating he told me that the two Miamians would sell the property back and leave Atlanta—if they could be granted a ninety-day temporary license while they "closed out their business." Well, we'd had a lot of experience with "temporary" licenses. They stretch out another ninety days, then six months, and the next thing you know political pressure enters into it and the temporary license becomes permanent. We were doing everything we could to keep anything that looked like a shady operation out of Atlanta, I told him, and as long as we had reason to suspect his clients there would be no license for them under any conditions. I had the total support on this of Alderman Richard Freeman, chairman of the police committee, and so I was confident that I could take a firm stand on the issue.

Apparently a lot of people were interested in seeing the opening of the Atlanta Raquet Club. On the Monday afternoon following the conversation with that lawyer, when the board of aldermen was in session and I was doing some work in my office, I had a long-distance call. It was from Jerome Cavanagh, the mayor of Detroit, a personal friend of mine. Jerry, who was president of the National League of Cities as well as the United States Conference of Mayors, said he wanted to come to Atlanta and see me. At this point he was being mentioned as a possible Democratic Party candidate for vice-president, and there was even some talk that he might become a candidate for president. I assumed he wanted to come so that he could assess his strength in the South.

"Fine," I said, "I'll set up a joint meeting of all the civic clubs in town, and you can address them."

"No, no," he said, "I want to see you about something personal, Ivan."

Something rang a bell. The Racquet Club. I suppose it was the fact that I'd had the thing on my mind so much lately. "Is it about some licenses?" I said.

"Two friends of mine from Miami don't feel they've been treated right in Atlanta."

"The Racquet Club?"

"Yes. They're really fine fellows, Ivan, and . . ."

"Jerry," I said. "You ought to see the FBI report."

"But if the record was *changed*."

"I don't see how you're going to change it."

"No, I mean if it could be shown that they're already licensed in Miami and Detroit and that they've got good reputations and they've done good honest business."

"Good reputations with *whom*, Jerry?"

"In business. Here and Miami."

"I just can't do it," I said. "Maybe if there was an error in the FBI report and it was changed, maybe we could reconsider. But I doubt it. These reports just don't have errors like that, Jerry, and you know it." Cavanagh wasn't too happy when we hung up.

I promised myself then that as long as Cavanagh and I were still in office I would never say anything beyond "no comment" about our conversation. Except among a few close personal friends I never said a thing except that the "mayor of one of the big cities" had called—I never used Cavanagh's name. But these things leak out, one way or another. I don't know whether I inadvertently said something, or the two men said something in Miami, or Cavanagh said something in Detroit, but several months later the FBI came to see me and asked if I would discuss the situation with them in detail—and confidentially—which I agreed to do, giving them all the information I had. And when the time came for Cavanagh to run again the story broke in the papers and the Detroit press tried everything it could to get me to make a statement linking Cavanagh to the attempt to open up the Atlanta Racquet Club in behalf of two rather questionable gentlemen from Miami.

# Riot

Hell-raisers of Summerhill,
And hell-raisers they were;
Every Friday and Saturday night,
There would surely be some fights . . .

—Black Atlanta folk singer
Tim Arkansaw,
"Hell-Raisers of Summerhill"

Then, in the midst of this dynamic period of growth—
"a brief sunlit hour, a time when hope and energy and
confidence flourished," *The New York Times* later called
it—there came the "long hot summers" of the mid-sixties.
While he was campaigning for the presidency in 1964
Barry Goldwater had pounded away at the rising crime
statistics in the country and coined the slogan "Crime in
the Streets," a coded rallying cry of the country's conservatives and a major issue in the campaign against Lyn-
don B. Johnson, and by the summer of 1966 Goldwater

was able to sit at home in Arizona and look at what was happening in cities all over the United States and smugly say, "I told you so." First there had been the uprising in Watts, the sprawling Negro ghetto in Los Angeles, and the flames had spread quickly over the rest of the country. Black residents of these oppressive slums were spilling into the sweltering streets of Newark and Detroit and Cleveland and Gary in a desperate revolt against ages of second-class citizenship. They had been shut off and forgotten in ghettos, without decent jobs and housing and educations and reasonable hope, and now they were assuming that the only way they would get anyone to recognize them and their problems was by rioting. It is possible that the single most dominant image we will have in later years to remind us of what it was like in the cities during the sixties will be a tragic montage of frustrated Negro rioters looting boarded-up stores and hurling Molotov cocktails and sniping from the tops of abandoned buildings, arrayed in their own neighborhood against fully armed white National Guardsmen crouching behind tanks in the middle of the glass-strewn streets, with sirens wailing and children crying and rifles snapping in the night, all of it ending as an entire section of the city smolders in the misty dawn of the morning after. Not only did the riots of the sixties take a terrible toll in lives and property, they also contributed heavily to the racial polarization already building to a head. "Crime in the Streets," as a code phrase for "keeping the nigger in his place," was soon to be replaced by more explicit slogans like "Law and Order" and "Support Your Local Police." Having law and order and supporting the police department are noble pursuits, but those weren't the issues at all. The real issue was whether we were going to get at the root *causes* of crime: the poverty and malaise that hovered over every ghetto neighborhood in the nation.

We had been lucky in Atlanta. The city was made up of better than 40 per cent Negro citizens (300,000 whites and some 200,000 blacks lived inside the city limits) and headquartered most of the civil-rights organizations, including the now-militant Student Nonviolent Coordinating Committee. The breaking down of the barriers of segregation had been too recent to give the black man in the streets time enough to rise above the poverty level, so we had our share of Negro slums and all of the attendant problems: fatherless homes, substandard housing, unemployment, ill health, and a general disaffection toward society. But we also had some things going for us that most cities did not have, and we counted on these to buy time for us while we tackled the basic causes. One of the most important factors in our favor was the large and responsible black-power structure made up of businessmen, academicians, and clergymen who, in the spirit of Martin Luther King, had patiently worked with the white leaders while we threw off our own prejudices and introduced ourselves to the problems of the Negro. Secondly, Atlanta was blessed with enough established Negro neighborhoods, places where many of the residents had grown up and now owned their own homes, in contrast to the typical crowded ghettos of the North that were populated with rootless migrants (*Southern* migrants, to be sure), to give us a more settled Negro community. Thirdly, and quite frankly, the Negro who had chosen to stay in the South, for better or for worse, had not yet reached the point of despair where he was ready to start burning down buildings and having it out in the streets with the National Guard or the city police. And, finally, there was a feeling, even in the darkest corners of our slums, that Atlanta was trying. We weren't doing enough, but we were trying.

Part of the faith the black people had in Atlanta was

directed toward me, I feel sure. They had seen a great breakthrough in civil rights during my first term in office, and they probably associated the desegregation efforts with me. Many of them had heard about the dinner for Dr. King, Jr. Many of them could see me almost any day of the week on a walking tour of the Negro slums. And of course I had gained great stature in the black community with my testimony in behalf of public accommodations. But beyond that we were beginning to take concrete action in cleaning up our slums and raising the level of living there. Atlanta was one of the first urban areas in the United States to receive a grant under the Economic Opportunity Act of 1964, and by the beginning of '66 Economic Opportunity Atlanta was starting to roll: a dozen neighborhood service centers, Head Start, Neighborhood Youth Corps, summer recreation, and other programs. Civic clubs, churches, and private groups were directing some attention toward clean-up drives and recreation facilities and employment. Community leaders, taking note of the rioting in other cities, began getting together at the grass-roots level to consider how they might avoid trouble in their own neighborhoods. And then in the summer of 1965 we created the Atlanta Commission on Crime and Juvenile Delinquency, a twenty-one-member blue-ribbon commission of black and white civic leaders from every walk of life, backed by hundreds of eager young attorneys, all of them donating their time and services for six months investigating the causes of crime in Atlanta. I should emphasize that *ostensibly* this was the object of the commission, for when its report came out in February 1966 —a 343-page book called *Opportunity for Urban Excellence*—it was anything but a simple document detailing crime in Atlanta. With the use of charts and graphs and interviews, as well as with letters from parents whose children had been in trouble, the commission had covered an incredibly wide range of problems: the court system, juvenile detention, alcoholism, housing, hunger, working mothers, low wages, drugs, *et al*, and had gone on to spell out hundreds of very specific recommendations. *Opportunity for Urban Excellence* pinpointed the city's troubled areas and made explicitly clear what we had vaguely paid lip service to for too long: that crime is merely the offspring of poverty. Using the report as our blueprint, we immediately set to work in all of the underprivileged areas of town, both black and white slums, and we had reason to feel that we were doing as much as any major city in America to help our poor onto their own feet and, consequently, avoid the outbreaks of violence many of the other cities were going through.

Still, we knew we were not immune. In spite of the prevalence of settled black neighborhoods that gave Atlanta's black community a degree of stability, we had a handful of less stable areas that I would frankly call ghettos. Atlanta, in a sense, is the South's Detroit and Chicago and New York. Atlanta is the mecca of the South not only to the ambitious young white person looking for excitement and advancement but also to the disenchanted Negro on a farm or in a tightly segregated town anywhere else in our part of the country. It is the "Dee-troit City" of the South, and almost every day of this century there has been the same hopeless sight of an illiterate, rootless, ill-fed, unskilled Negro coming into the big city from a farm in south Alabama, without money, without family, without connections, without any hope whatsoever of finding so much as a night's meal. He was coming into Atlanta to find . . . what? Usually to find loneliness like he never knew existed, and hunger and extreme poverty and no decent work he could do, usually to wind up on the city's relief rolls or in prison or dead from a Friday-night cutting. I was always able to sympathize with John

V. Lindsay in New York and Richard Daley in Chicago and Jerome Cavanagh in Detroit when they talked about how their problems had been inherited from the South, because many of Atlanta's human problems of the past few decades were originally the problems of the Black Belt. At any rate, Atlanta had its share of dispossessed Negro migrants from the farmed-out regions of the South; and when they showed up in the city they tended to move onto the same rundown ghetto block where their buddy from down home had moved, and suddenly we had large pockets of these rootless, hopeless people who felt no regard for anything beyond the next meal and had (we knew too well they had) the capacity for spontaneous violence.

Summerhill was ideal for a riot in Atlanta, if one were to happen. At one time this had been a fairly elegant section of town, consisting of roomy two-story white frame houses and shady streets and sidewalks, which before World War II had been populated by large well-to-do white families with enough time and money to make it one of Atlanta's nicest close-in neighborhoods, only eight or ten blocks from the Capitol and a short trolley ride to the downtown business area. But after the war these more substantial white families began moving out of the area, to be followed first by lower-class whites and finally by blacks. And by the sixties the area, now called Summerhill, was a teeming black ghetto. There were around ten thousand poor Negroes crammed into 354 acres. The once graceful homes that had housed single families were now chopped up into "apartments," sometimes a dozen to each house, and the grass was gone from the lawns and the screens were hanging from the windows and the plaster was falling from the ceilings and the paint was peeling from the walls. Almost every new resident who came in was a migrant without a job or money, with little hope of finding either. The majority of the families consisted of a working mother, if she could find somebody to look after her large brood of children, and no legal father. The Atlanta Commission on Crime's report had shown that Summerhill ranked tops in every category: juvenile delinquency, rape, robbery, aggravated assault, murder, *et al.* It was a tinderbox of poverty, disease, crime, frustration, and unrest, sitting in the very shadow of our new stadium, and no matter what we did it was like putting a Band Aid on a cancer. We knew that one spark could touch off a riot in Summerhill just as it had in Hough and Watts and all of the other similar ghettos in the rest of the country. We prayed a lot for rain on those sweltering summer weekend nights of 1966 in Summerhill, where nearly twenty per cent of the people were out of work.

We made it through the summer without incident, but ahead of us was September, which in the South can be, with its long days of interminable heat, even more conducive to violence in a condensed area than summer itself. And besides, on the day after Labor Day, I had enough trouble on my hands already. For one thing, the board of aldermen was still in session trying to work something out over a controversial proposal to increase water bills fifty per cent with a sewer service charge. And for another, we had a strike of city firemen still going on after several weeks—about 600 out of a force of 850 men were on strike —and I was up to here in negotiations. With that strike on, in the back of my mind was the chilling question of what in the world would happen if a riot broke out and fire bombs started flying. Anyway, at 4 o'clock that afternoon I was in my office talking on the phone with the labor lawyer representing the striking firemen when Captain George Royal rushed in breathlessly and blurted, "My God, Mr. Mayor, a riot!"

My heart hung in my throat. "What?"

"There's people all over the place. Capitol and Ormond."

"Summerhill?"

"Yes, sir. Right down from the stadium."

"Carmichael down there?"

"He was. What do you want to do?"

I didn't have to think about it. "I'm going down there," I said. Royal had a shocked look on his face, but I didn't give him a chance to argue. We took the steps two at a time down to the basement, jumped into the car, and screeched off toward Summerhill.

When the first of the big-city riots had taken place, I had begun doing all of the studying I could and trying to come up with a contingency plan of my own in case the trouble spread to Atlanta. It was obvious that cities and their police departments are not equipped to handle things like this all by themselves. There had never been a riot in Atlanta, just as there had never been a riot in Los Angeles before Watts, and a police department singularly effective in carrying out the normal duties of law enforcement—supervising traffic, maintaining order, those basic things a police department is supposed to do—can also be singularly incapable of controlling a riot. The main problem is a shortage of personnel. Atlanta, for instance, had a police force totaling near a thousand men; there were never more than three hundred on duty at any one time, and marshaling the other seven hundred at a moment's notice would take some doing. So I had made two specific moves in advance of any riot that might occur. First I had prepared a list of the twenty-five leading Negro ministers in the city and made a verbal agreement with them that this list would be distributed to the Police Department and in case of an emergency the police would immediately pick up the ministers and bring them to me;

the idea being that the ministers might be able to reason with a mob when no one else could. Secondly, I had arranged with Governor Sanders to get the help of the state highway patrol if I asked for it; but without undue encroachment on the city, meaning the troopers would be under the city's orders and not the state's.

And there was still another move I was sure I would make if bad trouble broke out: I would go to the heart of the riot and physically expose myself. I had realized for a couple of years, ever since my civil-rights testimony in Washington, that I was regarded as one of the champions of the civil-rights cause by both sides. The conservatives and the racists were holding me responsible for whatever might go wrong after the granting of civil rights to the Negro; something that was unfair to me, I think, but a reality just the same. And the liberals and the blacks would be more likely to listen to me than they would to most leaders, I felt, if I showed to them that I had the courage of my convictions by walking into the middle of a dangerous situation. Also, I had seen how the rioters had gotten all of the attention from the media in other cities—the police and the city government always came out looking like the ones in the wrong. I was determined that I would be there right alongside *my* police department and that I was going to be as much a part of the media picture on the right side as I considered the rioters to be on the wrong side. I had made up my mind that summer what I would do in case of trouble, and I remember telling my wife Louise, "If trouble breaks out, it's going to break out over me."

So as Captain Royal and I raced toward Summerhill I had time to think about what I was going to do when we got there, and to find out more from him about what had touched off the trouble. Late that morning I had been visited by Stokely Carmichael, who was still with the

Student Nonviolent Coordinating Committee. He came to the office at City Hall with a group of young black people to protest the mass arrest some days earlier of an antiwar group that had tried to break into the Army induction center on Ponce de Leon Avenue. Although Carmichael refused to shake hands with me and ranted and raved about "police brutality" and then attempted to block the entrance to the mayor's office, it was not what I would call a confrontation; it was just the sort of incident we had begun to get used to, which I tried to dismiss as smoothly as possible. As it turned out, that was only the beginning of the day for Carmichael in Atlanta. Early in the afternoon a young black man wanted for automobile theft was spotted by an Atlanta police detective cruising through Summerhill, and when the man was placed under arrest he broke away from the police officer and was shot in the leg trying to run away. This, of course, is the gray area of law enforcement: do you just let people run, or do you try to enforce the law? I don't say the law has been fairly enforced in the South for all of these years. I don't think it always has been. Maybe in a lot of cases a black man has been shot when a white man wouldn't have been. Anyway, the decision of the officer was to assert his authority, and I have never questioned his decision: he called for the suspect to stop, the man did not stop, the officer shot him in the leg to stop him, and the fat was in the fire. Carmichael and some of his crowd heard about the incident immediately and within minutes were cruising Summerhill in a SNCC sound truck, broadcasting all kinds of lies to stir the residents up. The wounded man had been rushed to Grady Hospital and given prompt medical attention and was not in a critical condition, but Carmichael's people were saying he had been murdered on his mother's front porch and that the people of Summerhill should revolt against "whitey" before "he kills us all." I don't think anything significant would have resulted if this had happened in any of the more stable neighborhoods, but this was a hot day after Labor Day in Summerhill—the porches and the yards and the sidewalks and the corner stores were crawling with aimless men and teen-agers looking for something to do —and Carmichael found a willing audience.

It became a classic demonstration of mob psychology, of how one person can mobilize a thousand others into a confused mass of bodies angrily flowing in all directions —and for what? They don't know. One reporter went around several hours later when things had died down and asked six people to give their version of what had started the trouble, and said he got six different versions that included a wildly imaginative tale of Atlanta policemen riding along in paddy wagons and picking people off with shotguns while they sat on their front porches.

When we reached Summerhill the police had already set up a roadblock at Capitol Avenue and Love Street, on the north edge of the slum and in sight of Atlanta Stadium. Two blocks down Capitol, at the bottom of the hill where the main avenue intersects with Ormond Avenue, a crowd of more than a thousand swirled around without direction in the bright late-afternoon sunlight. Some cars in the vicinity of Capitol and Ormond had been turned over and burned, and the sunlight was picking up reflections from bits of shattered glass on the sidewalks and in the street. The small number of policemen who had arrived on the scene had been forced to pull back from the center of the riot area. About half a dozen of them, under Captain Oscar Jordan, were regrouping at the roadblock when Royal and I screeched to a halt and got out of the car. I wore a simple conservative gray business suit and a gray tie. I guess the color of my face matched.

"Captain Jordan, is the chief here yet?" I said.

"No, Sir, not yet."

"All right, until he arrives I'm in charge."

"Yes, Sir, Mr. Mayor."

"Let's go, George." Royal and I started walking down the hill, headed for the center of the trouble.

"What are you going to do?" said Captain Jordan.

"I'm going to walk through the damned thing."

"Mayor, you can't go down there."

"Oscar," I said, "don't start telling me what to do."

By this time George Royal had radioed word for Ann Moses to send for the twenty-five Negro ministers and to advise Governor Sanders that I wanted at least two hundred state troopers immediately. The police were beginning to react now, wheeling into the area from all directions with their blue lights flashing, setting up other roadblocks and starting to move in and cut off and contain the trouble so it couldn't spread to other sections. We found ourselves, again, trying to buy time. Carmichael and his associates had, predictably, left the scene. Now the job was to keep the trouble in Summerhill and try to reason with the crowd. We didn't want a show of force—not yet, not unless it became necessary, only as a last resort. We wanted to divide the mob and find the leaders, and then find out whether they would listen to the black ministers when they got there. So here we went, George Royal and I in business suits, now joined by a bright young uniformed officer named Morris Redding—none of us wearing any sort of protection in case bricks or bottles or worse started flying—three well-fed white men strolling down the street into a howling mob of disenchanted and confused black people.

I don't think I could ever relate my exact feelings. I knew a knife could be stuck into me and nobody would ever know who did it. I knew I could be pounced upon and trampled. I knew I could be hit by a brickbat flying from a hedge. I knew I could be shot from a second-story window. With every step I became less confident that I was going to be able to do any good. I could smell whiskey as I walked past the people who were laying back on the edge of the fracas. I could see a certain wild look in their eyes, the look of somebody who has quit caring. And I could not find a single familiar face. These were clearly the migrants we had charted in our studies of crime in Atlanta. Here was a gray-haired middle-aged man who was walking unarmed onto their "turf," somebody in a good suit and good shoes who represented The Man to them, somebody who must be crazy for just coming right into their midst like that without a gun or anything. I was scared, but that didn't occur to me until after it was all over. You finally go with your instincts. You finally reach a point in a situation like this where you have to throw discretion aside and get on with it.

It seemed like everybody in the crowd saw us at once. A relative hush fell over them, they were so caught off guard for something like this to happen, and as we kept walking slowly down the middle of the street we could see some of the apparent leaders slinking off to the periphery and as we got closer and closer the crowd parted as though there were ropes on either side holding them back from us. I'm certain that most of them had no idea who I was. Now and then one of them would jump out in front of us and yell or make faces or challenge us, but we would quietly say, "Excuse me," and quickly slip around them to avoid a confrontation. We were being spat upon, but no one touched us or jostled us. As we would pass, the shouting would pick up again in waves behind our backs, but it was clear that our strategy had broken their momentum while also buying us a little more time.

The next thing I knew, we had walked through the crowd and were standing virtually alone in the middle of

the street about a hundred feet up the hill from the intersection where the trouble was centered. From that van-
tage point I could see the scene as a whole for the first
time. Below me was the crowd, which had begun to swirl
back and forth again after getting over its shock at seeing
the three of us walk into their midst. Little black children
were flitting about on the fringes, laughing and yelling
and having the time of their lives. Some of the more concerned residents of the area had taken their children and
gone inside their houses, and were peeking through cur-
tains. It was impossible to pinpoint all of the leaders of
the mob, though here and there I could find one (they
were the younger ones, the firebrands with Afro hair-
cuts and blue jeans and ragged sneakers) raising his
clenched fist and exhorting the small audience he had
been able to muster. And I could look all the way up
Capitol Avenue, toward the stadium, where that first
roadblock had been, and see those blessed blue lights of
police cars flashing on the horizon as the Atlanta Police
Department began to organize. I knew that the organization would begin to function and the periphery would
begin to close up, and that perhaps some of those police
cars were bringing the black ministers I so badly wanted
right now. And I knew that the mob had no sense of the
total picture, no sense of time, no general plan such as
ours. We stood there for a minute or two and then I said,
"Let's go back."

How many times we walked back and forth through
that crowd, I will never know. Soon I was aware that
word was spreading about who I was. "It's the mayor,"
somebody would say, and there would be a ripple in the
crowd as the news was passed along. I began trying to
get to some of the older ones by touching them lightly on
the elbow or shoulder and saying, "Come on, let's go
home; let's try to work this out without anybody getting

hurt." Some would listen to me, drifting away to where they lived or at least moving off the street to somebody's yard or porch, others would jerk away and start shouting. At one point I saw a young man who had a pack of Winstons in a see-through summer shirt pocket (I never carried cigarettes, but took to bumming them when I became nervous), and I looked him right in the eye and said, "Give me a cigarette." He was so stunned, I think, that he mechanically handed me the whole pack. "Give me a match," I said, but by that time he had recovered and snatched the pack away from me. "I ain't giving you no match, *too*," he said. Then, for a brief moment, I thought I had them. We had been walking back and forth like that for what seemed like forty-five minutes or an hour and I had two or three of the young leaders following after me and I turned to them and proposed taking the entire crowd to the stadium to talk it over. "You can elect some leaders, and I'll take them over to City Hall, and we'll sit down and discuss your grievances and your problems, and we'll see if we can help you." They went for the idea, and we started on up Capitol Avenue toward the stadium. I felt like the Pied Piper with hundreds of people starting to fall in behind me, and as I was waving ahead for the police to move the blockades out of the way, the SNCC leaders who had stayed around to see what they had wrought descended on me. "We ain't going to no goddam white man's stadium . . . They'll get you in there and the po-*lee*ces will shoot you down . . . Ain't nothing but a white man's trick . . . Get the white honky bastards before they get you . . ." And I found I had lost them just when I thought I had won them.

All of our efforts at reasoning with the crowd went downhill from that point. Somehow a police car had gotten right into the middle of the intersection at Capitol and Ormond, and when the crowd left me it swarmed around the car and the car became the very center of everything. There were about two thousand people around the car. Some bricks were being thrown and there was a pulsation—a fever—in the mob that had not been there before. We knew we had to do something fast. So far we had been able to keep them moving, keep them divided, but now they were together, and it was a dangerous situation. Somebody said I should get on top of the police car and try to talk to them, so I was handed a bullhorn and boosted up on the hood, and I struggled to the roof of the car while the crowd alternately cheered and jeered. I knew I had made a serious tactical mistake the minute I stood atop that car, alone and vulnerable and exposed, a prosperous-looking Northside businessman with a good suit and well-tanned cheeks, looking down at a mob of two thousand people taunting me and zeroing in on me. When I was unable to do any good with them I happened to spot a responsible-looking black man in a clerical collar, and I said to him, "Reverend, will you get up here and pray?" But when I had helped him on top of the car and handed him the bullhorn he went off onto a wild tear, haranguing the crowd and mocking me (three years later this same man ran for public office in Atlanta and was roundly defeated). Then a militant young man in a stained sweatshirt, one of the SNCC leaders, grabbed the bullhorn and started chanting, "Black Power, Black Power, Black Power," and the crowd began rocking the car, and the crescendo was shattering. People were yelling, "Black Power!" and I was alone atop the police car, and the crowd was surging in on me and some bricks began to fly and just as I was jitterbugging and about to lose my balance I simply dived off the car into the arms of Morris Redding and George Royal.

We tried to resume walking back and forth through the crowd, foolishly thinking we still had a chance to disperse it, but it was all over now. A policeman had tried to stop some kids from looting a candy machine in the service station on the corner, and several people had moved in on him; Redding, Royal, and I ran over and broke it up. Up the street one of the press photographers had been badly hurt by a brick that had been tossed into the crowd. Bricks and bottles were beginning to sail from behind houses and bushes and trees now, and this is when I lost all restraint. I saw a group of people pounce on one of the policemen, who had begun to move with force, and it was then that I gave the order to use the tear gas.

Although most of my actions were instinctive, when I look back I think I would do everything exactly as I did that afternoon, with the possible exception of getting on top of the police car. We had done everything humanly possible that the top officials of a city could do in a crisis like that. We had tried to reason with the crowd. We had exposed ourselves to them. The police had restrained themselves one hundred per cent until there was no other recourse but to show their strength and try to take command of the situation before it got entirely out of hand. The police quickly took over, firing their pistols into the air and unleashing the tear gas and at the same time tightening the noose around Summerhill to completely seal it off. People, myself included, were being knocked to the ground by the tear gas. Children could be heard choking and wailing inside the houses in the bottoms, where the gas clung to the ground like thick fog. The police had gotten an armored car into the area (the first time they had ever had to use it) and were inching toward the main intersection. At one point I thought I was leading a charge up a short side street to clean out some of the brick- and bottle-throwers, but when I looked back I saw only Royal and Redding trying to catch up with me. It was not what we would have preferred to do, use our police power to put down the trouble, but it was our only alternative after a point and when we moved we moved with authority. The crowd broke up quickly after the tear gas had been put to work. Amazingly, no one was killed. When the black ministers began to gather around me I took them to the scattered groups of people still milling around the intersection, and they tried to get them to go home ("Mayor, we don't know these people," one of the preachers said). Finally, when it appeared we had everything under control, I felt a firm hand on my arm and looked up to see Chief Jenkins. "For God's sake, Mr. Mayor, you've hit a home run," he said. "Now get out of here and get straightened out while you've got the chance." He put me in his car and whisked me back to City Hall. More than one hundred state-highway patrolmen had gathered out of sight in a tunnel at the stadium, but it looked like we wouldn't be needing them now.

Louise was there when I reached the office. After I stripped off the soaking wet clothes and took a shower and calmed down a bit I sat down with her and tried to tell her everything that had happened. She had suffered a great deal that day, sitting at home and watching some of it on television, unable to do anything else. Then I got back in the car and returned to Summerhill, to stand on the corners with the police and press at nightfall. Everything was quiet now. Whiffs of tear gas still could be smelled in the low areas. The lights of police cruisers picked up glints from the bits of shattered glass littering the streets. I could see the blue-white lights coming from television sets inside most of the houses and shabby rooms, and knew the people of Summerhill were going through the eerie experience of watching themselves on the network news shows, watching the tragic play of brick-throwing and gun-firing, watching their mayor as he was shaken off the top of an automobile, watching their neighborhood as it was turned into a battleground—and I hoped it would have as sobering an effect on all of those frustrated people inside those ragged houses as it had on me. On the streets of Summerhill that night I was button-holed for interviews by the national news media, wanting to know if there was any way this could have been pre-vented. "Yes," I said, "had we started a hundred years ago making the necessary corrections, and had the wis-dom in America then not to let these slums become the places they are . . ." We had said it many times before, and we had meant it, but never with the conviction that we had that night as Summerhill and the rest of Atlanta drifted off into a fitful sleep.

# Martin Luther King, Jr.

> Ivan, the minute they bring King's body back
> tomorrow—between then and the time of the
> funeral—Atlanta, Georgia, is going to be the
> center of the universe.
>
> —Robert W. Woodruff,
> developer of Coca-Cola,
> on the night of King's assassination

Over the years I developed a close and warm friendship with Dr. Martin Luther King, Sr., an association that began during the sit-ins at Rich's when Dr. King was one of the two dozen Negro leaders meeting regularly with Opie Shelton and me in trying to work out the desegregation of stores and lunch counters in the downtown area. He worked hard for my support in both of my campaigns and eventually became a confidant of mine, someone who was always ready with steadying advice whenever I needed it, particularly about racial matters and the temperament of the black community. We were together on hundreds of occasions during those trying times: at bond-issue meetings, commission hearings, civil-rights confrontations, and numerous banquets and other social functions. He was one of the strongest and most faithful representatives of Atlanta's black people, and our friendship held up even when I refused to back my vice-mayor —and the Negro community's choice—to succeed me.

But it was not until the Nobel Prize dinner at the Dinkler Hotel in Atlanta that I began to get to know Dr. King's son, Martin Luther King, Jr. Later that same year I was invited to New York to attend a national meeting of the American Jewish Committee, which was putting on an elegant dinner in honor of Dr. King, Jr. Morris Abram, the former Atlanta attorney who had killed the county-unit system and had been sent by President Kennedy to ask me to testify in behalf of the public-accommodations bill, was president of the Committee that year and, of course, a great friend of the younger King. There were about two thousand leading Jewish citizens there that night from all over the nation, and in his introduction Abram spoke of the friendship shared by three men from contrasting backgrounds: himself, a Jewish boy raised in south Georgia; Dr. King, a black child out of a segregated Southern city; and myself, from slave-owning grandparents and the privileged white business class. And when Martin Luther King, Jr., got up he acknowledged my presence and said he had never thought as a young boy growing up in a segregated community that he would be honored by a group like this in New York City. "But adding to the honor," he said, "is the fact that I have been accompanied here by the mayor of Atlanta, Georgia: my good and close friend, Ivan Allen, Jr." The applause equaled anything I had heard during my stay in office. I didn't know what to do. Someone indicated that I should stand up. The applause continued. I sat down, then stood up again. I was at a loss for words. After all I had been through on the racial issue, Martin Luther King, Jr., had made a point of recognizing my contribution.

I mention these things merely to show that Dr. King and I had a relationship that was slow and late in blooming, mainly because I was up to my ears with the daily routine in Atlanta's City Hall, and he was trying to carry the civil-rights cause to every corner of the nation. The relationship was solid and based on a mutual respect and admiration for each other's problems and accomplishments. Many times when he was in town I would drop by the SCLC offices on Auburn Avenue, and we would have frank informal discussions that might last the better part of a day: he filling me in on the national racial picture, I telling him what was happening or was going to happen in Atlanta. On one of those visits, in 1967, he gave me a copy of his book, *Where Do We Go from Here: Chaos or Community?*, autographed it, and then drove me back in his car and dropped me off at City Hall. I don't read nearly as much as I should, but I found myself constantly referring to that book. Many of the paragraphs have been marked, such as one on page 10: "Every civil rights law is still substantially more dishonored than honored. School desegregation is still 90 per cent unimplemented across the land, the free exercise of the franchise is the exception rather than the rule in the South. Open occupancy laws theoretically apply to population centers, embracing tens of millions, but grim ghettos contradict the fine language of the legislation." Unconsciously, I was using the book as an extension of the chats I had had with him—as a sort of White Paper to guide me in whatever I did as mayor. Martin Luther King, Jr., had become to me, as he had to millions of people all over the world, the personification of the fight to gain equality for all people.

On the night of Thursday, April 4, 1968, Louise and I were in our bedroom at home watching television and reading the newspaper when a bulletin flashed on the screen: MARTIN LUTHER KING, JR., SHOT IN MEMPHIS. The second I saw it I jumped to my feet and said, "Good God, won't they ever learn? First Kennedy, now King!" It is hard to describe the feeling I had. I suppose millions of others all over the world had the same feeling of shock and anger at that same second. Dr. King had been in Memphis during a sanitation workers' strike and was just getting ready to go out to dinner with some of the other SCLC workers when a shot rang out and dropped him on the balcony of the Lorraine Motel. Instinctively, I called Ann Moses and got the Kings' home telephone number from her and dialed it. Mrs. King answered. I had moved so fast I didn't know whether she had even been told of the shooting yet.

"Have you heard about Dr. King?" I said.

She seemed composed. "I just talked to Memphis."

"What do you want to do?"

"I'm going up there right now."

"Is there anything I can do for you?"

"There's a plane leaving in about fifty minutes, and I would appreciate your help in getting me on it." I told her I would send a police car after her, and that I would be there myself as soon as I could, and we hung up. At this point all of my responses were as a friend of the King family rather than as mayor of Atlanta. From my brief conversation with Mrs. King, I gathered that her husband was not in serious condition because she had just talked to someone in Memphis and seemed steady. Even so, she needed friends with her and her children. I arranged to have a police car rushed to the King home and quickly put on a shirt and tie.

"What are you going to do?" Louise said.

"I'm going to Mrs. King."

"I'll get a coat. I'm going with you." A woman could help more than a man, she knew. We hurried outside into the drizzling rain and got into our Chevrolet (this was one of the few times in my eight years that I had not come home in the radio-equipped city car, leaving me without communications when I needed it the most), and slithered onto Northside Drive, racing through the wet night to find the King home. As we turned off Northside onto Magnolia Street and screeched through the heart of Vine City, a poorly lighted black neighborhood that was still one of our difficult areas, I had my first qualms about bringing Louise with me. It was the first time I had any thoughts about the situation the entire nation was going to be faced with for the next week or so. *What must they be thinking in those narrow, cluttered frame houses?* First there had been John Kennedy, and now, less than four years later, their greatest champion of all had been gunned down. What were the black people in Martin Luther King's hometown going to do if his wounds turned out to be fatal? I had great apprehension as we screeched onto Sunset. Here was a middle-aged white couple from Northside Drive, moving through the center of Vine City on a dark night in an unmarked car with no protection only an hour after the hero of the black people had been shot. I was praying for the best, remembering what Martin had said that night at the Wheat Street Baptist Church—"If anyone breaks this contract, let it be the white man"—but I must admit I couldn't blame the people of Vine City for whatever actions they might take in retaliation.

When we reached the King home, the police car was out front and Mrs. King was coming down the steps. Reverend and Mrs. Fred Bennette and Mrs. Sam Williams were already there. They put Coretta in the front seat of the two-door police car and I was already in the back seat when I realized I still had not called the airline to hold the 8:25 plane to Memphis, and I wouldn't be able to use the radio from the back seat. Just as we were preparing to leave for the airport, George Royal drove up in another police car and I jumped in beside him. So, with Mrs. King in one police car and me in another and Louise and Mrs. Williams in our personal car, we roared off toward the airport.

It was then, when I had given positive orders for the airline to hold the plane for Mrs. King, that I began to sense my larger reponsibilities; that I had to act not only because I was a personal friend of Martin and Coretta King but also because I was the mayor of Atlanta. The death of Dr. King would not only be a personal tragedy, it would be a tragedy for the nation and for the South and for Atlanta. I tried to ask myself what John F. Kennedy would have done at a time like this. Having lived with the problems in the ghettos during 1966 and 1967, being quite aware of the tender feelings in the cities all over America then, I knew that even if Martin lived there would possibly still be major rioting in Atlanta. Dr. King, as the leader of the nonviolent movement, wouldn't want it that way, of course; but that was beside the point. I wanted to do whatever I could to assure the black people of Atlanta that we *cared,* that Martin Luther King was also *our* friend. As a starter, I got back on the police radio and placed call after call to the police dispatcher, giving the car number and saying this was Mayor Allen and letting it be known that I was with Mrs. King and was escorting her to the airport. I wanted the news media to know, so that information would get out to all of those bleak Negro homes: Atlanta cares, Atlanta is doing whatever it can. There had been nothing in my past experience to prepare me to handle a situation like this. Again, there are times when you have to go with your instincts. This was another of those times.

The police had their instincts working, too, and that made me feel stronger as I tried to guess at what the next few days would hold for them. Four of us in particular —Chief Jenkins, George Royal, Morris Redding and I—had been inseparably tied together by the problems of the civil-rights movement during the decade, and our mutual friendship and understanding had reached such a point that we could almost always anticipate the others' moves. I found that each of us that night were instinctively taking the actions we would have taken if we had been able to sit down and write out a lengthy plan. First, I had rushed to Mrs. King's side as soon as I heard of the shooting in Memphis. Chief Jenkins, realizing that he was second in command and that the second danger spot in the city that night would be the elder Kings' home, went immediately to see that Martin's parents were protected. George Royal, now promoted to superintendent, knew I would first go to Mrs. King's, and he rushed there to give any assistance he could. And Morris Redding, who was now my aide, didn't have to think twice about going directly to the airport where he knew I would be. None of us had been in communication with the other. It was as though we had rehearsed it.

Morris Redding and Jack Nelson of the *Los Angeles Times'* regional bureau were already waiting when we arrived at the airport. While the Bennettes helped Mrs. King out of one car, I got out of mine and grabbed Redding by the arm and handed him two hundred dollars. "Morris," I told him, "for God's sake get two tickets for Memphis." I hadn't made up my mind yet whether I should stay in Atlanta or accompany her to Memphis (although I think I would have gone with her if Martin had lived), but I still had enough presence of mind to get tickets for the flight. I guess the customs of a lifetime stick with us: here I was worrying about *buying* tickets, no matter what the emergency was. Other newsmen were beginning to reach the airport as we started down the ramps, looking for the right Eastern Airlines gate. As soon as we found the gate and were about to turn into the waiting room, Dora McDonald, Dr. King's executive secretary, came running after us. She seemed extremely upset. She grabbed Mrs. King and said, "Coretta, we've got to go in here," and pulled her into the adjoining ladies' restroom. At the same instant an Eastern official came up to me and said, "They've got to talk to you over the telephone."

I expected the worst, from the look on Dora McDonald's face. I went to the nearest phone. It was someone identifying himself as an Eastern official.

"Mayor Allen?"

"Yes, this is Ivan Allen, Jr."

"I've been asked to inform you that Dr. King is dead."

I had to be sure. "I want you to go back and reaffirm your statement and be positive that this is right."

"Mayor Allen," he said, "I have been instructed to affirm and *reaffirm* to you that Dr. King is dead."

I was numb. When I came out of the phone booth I saw Louise, who had not been able to keep up with the two police cars going to the airport. She saw the look on my face. We walked over to Dora and Coretta, who had their arms around each other and were standing in the middle of the corridor now. I felt certain Coretta knew her husband was dead, but it was my duty to tell her officially. I was grateful that there were two women with her the moment I had to tell her. I said, "Mrs. King, I have to inform you that Dr. King is dead."

I don't remember that she said anything. Certainly, she had trained herself for the possibility of that moment in all of those years while Martin exposed himself to crowds of rednecks in angry small Southern towns. She had been able to steel herself for it in the few minutes she was with Dora and I was on the phone, when it was fairly obvious what the news was. Hearing it said for the first time was something else, though. The four of us stood there for what seemed like an eternity, holding hands, Coretta showing great courage and dignity and poise.

"Coretta," I said, "do you want to go to Memphis, or what?"

"I can't help in Memphis," she said. "My place tonight is with my children." She was right.

After I notified Eastern to release the plane, we went back through the airport. I don't remember that walk. The press had started to catch up with us by then, and a couple of television cameras were grinding away. The cars had been brought around to a rear gate. It was raining hard now. We got into the cars and took the interminable drive back to the King house, in silence. I held an umbrella for Coretta and helped her into the house. We had been gone for about an hour and fifteen minutes, and by this time a large contingent of Atlanta police had arrived to guard the house and the children, and a number of friends, black and white, had come to do whatever they could. Coretta retired to her bedroom, and all of us were left in the front rooms, shocked and dazed. There was a phone call to Mrs. King from President Johnson. Then the President was on television, and that was an eerie feeling—to be sitting in the house of Martin Luther King, Jr., watching the President talk to the nation about what a tragedy had just taken place. Finally we left for City Hall.

By the time I got to my office, around ten o'clock that night, it was already the center of attention. Ann Moses, working on instinct, as the rest of them had been doing since the first announcement of Dr. King's shooting, had rushed down to open up the office, and when we arrived there it was jammed with newsmen trying to find out what I had done and what I planned to do. Riots had already broken out in several cities over the country. The obvious question was, would there be trouble in Atlanta, Martin Luther King's birthplace? By now, that was the major question in my mind. Could we hold together that huge Atlanta University complex on the west side of the city, the six predominantly Negro universities and colleges— Martin's alma mater, Morehouse College, among them —from whence had come the front-line soldiers in the civil-rights crusade? Without a doubt, the world had already shifted its attention from Memphis to Atlanta. The body would be brought back here, and it would be put into the ground here.

Still in somewhat of a daze, I first put together a proclamation deploring the assassination and calling for level-headed citizens to act properly and show their respect for Martin Luther King, Jr. I wouldn't say it was one of the greater proclamations, but we were under too great a strain to operate effectively on things like that. Then I began sending for my aides, the people closest to me, the ones I could depend upon to get the machinery rolling: Earl Landers, my administrative assistant; Milton Farris, chairman of the Aldermanic Finance Committee; Henry Bowden, the city attorney; Herbert Jenkins, George Royal, Morris Redding, Ann Moses. Telephone calls were coming in and going out. I kept calling the news media, keeping them posted on everything that was happening. I stayed in touch with the educators at Atlanta University to keep abreast of their situation.

We had to be realistic about it. There would likely be serious trouble, particularly in the black neighborhoods. Milton Farris never raised a question when I told him we would have to put the police department on double shifts, something we were allowed to do only on the most extreme provocation. I was asking him to call in every policeman in Atlanta and run two twelve-hour shifts. That could get very expensive, and Farris knew as well as I that we would be damned if we did and damned if we didn't: we would be assailed by that same crowd of haters for bending over backwards to help the Negro or, if no trouble broke out, for wasting thousands of the taxpayers' dollars. But Milton never raised an eyebrow when I requested the double shifts: "Whatever you think is right, it should be done." It was a difficult thing to do. You can't work men for twelve hours a day, seven days a week, for very long. There was no quibbling from Farris or from Chief Jenkins.

Then, about midnight, I finally got in a call to the President. This was the only time in my eight years as mayor that I called the President of the United States. I simply wanted him to know that the leadership in Atlanta, Dr. King's home, was alerted to the dangers and aware of the magnitude of the situation. I guess I just wanted to talk to the President. At any rate, President Johnson returned the call within minutes. It was obvious to me that he and Mrs. Johnson had already retired for the night when I placed my call.

"What does it look like down there?" he said.

"It's all right, right now, Mr. President," I told him. "I'm worried, but I'm hopeful. It's raining pretty hard, and that's a big help. It'll keep people off the streets."

"We've had a lot of rioting in the country."

"That's what we heard."

"We've had to commit a lot of troops already."

"Yes, sir."

"I'll do whatever's necessary, Mayor," he said, "but this stuff is breaking out all over. I hope we don't have to send anybody down there. I hope if it gets bad in Atlanta the National Guard can take care of it."

It was a soothing conversation. President Johnson was as cool as he could be. He impressed me as being a tough man when the chips are down, and the way he handled it helped settle my nerves. Then he put Mrs. Johnson on the phone and she spoke to me, recalling a visit she had made to Atlanta and expressing her sympathy over Dr. King's death and saying their prayers were with us. Only someone who had been through those past few hours could have appreciated what that phone call meant to me.

Then, just as I was preparing to leave City Hall to go home for some sleep, I had a long distance call. I don't think I was quite aware yet just how big this situation really was. I hadn't had time to think about what was going to happen tomorrow or the next day; I was trying to make it through this one. The call was from Robert Woodruff, the developer of Coca-Cola, one of Atlanta's staunchest citizens, the man who had done more to help build and direct Atlanta during the past thirty years than any one person. Woodruff had been, during my six years, my most valued unofficial advisor. He had called me on several occasions, whenever Atlanta was going through traumatic experiences, not to give me advice but to give me suggestions on the nature of the problem and what could possibly be done. The advice he had given me on whether or not I should go to testify in behalf of the public-accommodations bill was something I could never fully thank him for, and typical of our relationship. Anyway, he was calling me after midnight from Washington. He and Carl Sanders had been paying a personal visit to the President at the White House when the announcement of the shooting came, and had retired to their hotel when news of the death was broadcast. And now he was saying, over long distance, "Ivan, how are things in Atlanta?"

"Calm right now, Mr. Woodruff." I filled him in on the situation and told him about the conversation with the President.

"I want to give you a little advice," he said.

"Yes, Sir."

"You've got to start looking ahead."

"They'll bring the body back tomorrow."

"I mean *really* look ahead, Ivan. The next four or five days. The problems you have tonight are nothing compared to what's ahead."

"Yes, Sir. We're doing what we can."

"Ivan," he said, "the minute they bring King's body back tomorrow—between then and the time of the funeral —Atlanta, Georgia, is going to be the center of the universe." He paused. "I want you to do whatever is right and necessary, and whatever the city can't pay for will be taken care of. Just do it right."

I got home around four o'clock in the morning, some nine hours after Louise and I had rushed away to be at the side of Mrs. King, and the wind had left me now. Robert Woodruff, I could see, had put it all in perspective. Atlanta *was* going to be the center of the world—"the center of the universe"—for the next few days. And in the spirit of those people who had selfishly made Atlanta into what it was, he was, in one breath, relieving me of any worries such as how we were going to pay for necessary police protection. I can't imagine the mayor of any other city in the United States being given a blank check like that, under such trying circumstances.

After a short, restless sleep I shook myself awake around seven o'clock the next morning. While I was having a cup of coffee the phone rang. It was Gene Patterson of the *Constitution*, who was complimentary over the way things had been handled the night before and wanted to know what my next moves would be. I told him I thought the key to the entire chain of events was what was going on at Atlanta University, and that I was going to try to set up a meeting that morning with the university presidents and be a part of whatever happened there. He thought it was a good idea.

"I'm going under one circumstance, though," I said.

"What's that?"

"That you'll go with me."

I heard the gasp. Patterson had always been an activist in the newspaper business, always wanting to be in the middle of things instead of sitting in an isolated editor's chair, but he was obviously reluctant to be put in the position of participating in the leadership—to commit himself to a course of action that might take some of his objectivity away from him. I think he realized the quandary I was in, though, and saw that the city needed all the help it could possibly get. He agreed to go.

We met with the Atlanta University leaders in one of the presidents' offices at nine-thirty that morning. They were as tired and sleepy-eyed as we were, and they didn't feel any better than they had the night before because nearly four thousand black students had notified them that they were going to have a march that morning in memory of Dr. King. This presented us with a familiar problem: do you give a permit, or do you refuse a permit? You have to ask yourself where lies the least chance for trouble. It finally boils down to making a basic decision —fish or cut bait—and reacting impulsively once more. I told the presidents I was going to back the march, to the point of asking if I could join the march, and I invited them to go with me.

To my amazement, the presidents advised me that they had never marched with their students throughout the civil-rights crusade—that it had always been their policy to stay in the background and only offer advice and that they didn't intend to change that policy now. A fierce debate followed. Then a secretary came into the room and said the students were getting ready to kick off their march. There had been no permit granted, but there was no way to control it by prohibiting it. Patterson and I stood up and said we were going down to participate in the march, and I asked them one last time to join us. To a man, they got up and followed us out of the room and across the campus to Hunter Street to join the students.

I walked up to a towering student, a young man about six feet, five inches tall, who appeared to be in charge, introduced myself, and told him I was deeply sympathetic and wanted to march with them. "Mayor Allen," he said, "we respect you, but this is a black man's march, and we don't want you to go with us." This frightened me, worried as I was that there was going to be a backlash on the part of the city's black community, but I couldn't afford a confrontation. He *did* say it would be all right to ride in a police car seventy-five to a hundred yards ahead of the marchers, gave me the line of march, and that is how Gene Patterson and I participated in it. For about an hour and a half we led the march across the west side of Atlanta, riding ahead in a police car. It was an orderly march, with no incidents of any kind—from the angered black students or from the whites lining the curbs here and there along the route.

As soon as I got back to City Hall it was time for a meeting of department heads that I had called that morning. The city was still orderly, and a fine drizzle was coming down. It was time for us to start laying plans for the funeral, which had been set for the following Tuesday. It had finally sunk in on us that this was not going to be merely a large funeral, or even a private funeral: it was going to be most public, and the people attending it would either be famous or emotional or both. Even so, we found ourselves that morning thinking in terms of a funeral procession of some ten thousand people. We still had not been able to grasp fully the magnitude of something like this. The death and the impending funeral of Martin Luther King, Jr., was easily the top story in the entire world, just as Robert Woodruff had predicted to me on the phone from Washington, but we couldn't see the forest for the trees. All we knew was what we read in the Atlanta papers; if, indeed, we even had time to do that. Even for a routine private funeral there are scores of minor details to be worked out in advance: the line of procession, the time, traffic police and so forth. For the King funeral (and, again, our estimate of the crowd at that point was only ten thousand), there would be endless other logistics: elimination of work crews on downtown streets, arrangements for press and network television crews, housing space for visitors, first-aid stations, extra police and firemen in case of trouble, even plans for the cleanup that would be required afterwards. We were confident we could handle the situation if we really went to work. We might not have been so confident if we had known how big it *really* was going to be.

I tried to get away for a game of golf at the Peachtree Golf Club Saturday morning with three friends. Dr. King's body had been brought back to the city Friday afternoon, and Sam Massell and I had been at the airport to meet it and Mrs. King, and ride along to the funeral home on Butler Street. Friday night had passed quietly, though there had been rioting all day in Washington and in many of the other Eastern cities, and the vanguard of those who would attend the funeral was beginning to reach Atlanta. After the golf game Saturday morning, our wives met us for lunch. I had been fidgety all morning. Something was bothering me, and I couldn't put my finger on it. I became so upset that I excused myself before lunch came and went back to my office, and then called another meeting of department heads.

This time we looked deeper into the entire situation, and the more we talked the more we were convinced that Atlanta was about to be the scene of the largest and most emotional funeral in the history of the United States. Reports kept trickling in from all over. Arrangements being made by the telephone company for phones and cables indicated there would be an unbelievable amount of coverage by the networks and the daily press. The SCLC was setting up an emergency headquarters, staffing it with scores of volunteers who were working around the clock to arrange for visitors from all over the world. The attorney general's office had sent in an advance detachment of men, apparently to lay some preliminary plans for security and to find out whether Atlanta's leaders were aware of the magnitude of the funeral. The department heads and I began raising our estimate on the size of the crowd expected for the funeral, from our first guess of ten thousand up to thirty thousand or more. There had still been no violence in Atlanta, but we knew full well that it was all ahead of us.

That night, I was still jumpy. I finally ended up calling Herbert Jenkins. Herbert and I had lived through many a crisis over the past several years, most of them related to civil rights, and he always had a settling effect on me: cool, level-headed, a good man to have around in an emergency, yet with an emotional pitch that gave him the capacity to understand problems of this type. I suggested that I run by and pick him up, and that the two of us just ride around town and see what was happening.

We decided to visit every Negro neighborhood in Atlanta, get out of the car at each one, and let ourselves be seen. We went to Summerhill, Vine City, Mechanicsville,

Pittsburg, Blue Heaven: all of them. Here we were, two white middle-aged gray-haired men—the mayor and the police chief of the city—walking up and down the streets, standing on the corners, talking to the people, trying to show them our concern. It was much the same strategy I had used during the rioting in Summerhill in 1966, and it seemed to be working. There were smiles and greetings from those who recognized us. And if you don't think word spreads like a brushfire in a black ghetto, you don't know much about that way of life. The grapevine, rather than newspapers or television or any other method of communication, is the traditional means of spreading the word there. I would dare say that by midnight, after Herbert and I had spent three or four hours simply showing ourselves in all the Negro areas of the city, more than half of Atlanta's black population of two hundred thousand knew what we had done.

Very late that night, when Herbert and I had hung around the busy Negro commercial section at Hunter and Ashby Streets and were about to call it quits, he told me SCLC had set up its communications headquarters in the West Hunter Street Baptist Church and suggested we drop by to see what was happening. I wanted to see the Reverend Ralph Abernathy, anyway. Ralph had been Dr. King's trusted right-hand man for all of those years, the heir apparent to the top job at SCLC now that Martin was gone, and this had thrown us together on many occasions. When Herbert and I entered the basement of the church, it was close to midnight, but the place was a beehive. Scores of workers, black and white, were talking on telephones and shuffling papers and making charts. We went over to Ralph and spoke to him for a few minutes, and then I pointed toward the bank of some thirty phones, each of them manned by a worker, and I said, "Who are these people talking to?"

"It's all long distance," Ralph Abernathy told me.

"Long distance?"

"Every one of them."

"Who the devil are they talking to?"

Ralph said, "People who're coming for the funeral."

"Do you mean to tell me . . . *all long distance?*"

"We're making arrangements with SCLC people all over the United States," he said. "We're setting up accommodations for people who're coming in for Tuesday."

When I looked around that room and saw thirty people on thirty telephones, talking to California and New York and Chicago and everywhere else you could imagine, the size of what was about to happen in Atlanta finally hit me in the head. To say that I was stunned and shocked would be putting it mildly. This wasn't any wild political headquarters. This was a massive, well-organized, highly supervised nerve center where plans were being made to receive as many as a hundred thousand people into Atlanta for one funeral. When Jenkins and I went outside, still trying to clear our heads, we were notified that a whiskey store just down the street had been broken into and that a gang of young Negroes had cleaned it out. Somehow, it didn't bother us. We were perfectly willing to sacrifice a couple of liquor stores.

Sunday morning, I was stalking back and forth in the kitchen like a caged animal. In the middle of the night I had gotten a call from Attorney General Ramsey Clark, who wanted to talk to me about the legal aspects of the funeral—the need for public facilities, even though officially this would be a private affair. "Look," he had said, "the Third Army is there [headquarters for the Third Army was at Fort McPherson in Atlanta], and I'm placing it at your disposal. Any help they can give you in the way of accommodations or anything, we'll see that they go all out." This had served to further heighten my apprehensions about our ability to cope with something this big, and I was pacing around the house when the phone rang on a private line. I don't know how he got the number, but it was a young minister named Randy Taylor from Central Presbyterian Church—a huge church across the street from City Hall, one that had managed to survive despite the fact that most of its congregation had moved away to the suburbs. Randy Taylor had called on me recently when he had come to Atlanta, and I vaguely recalled our meeting. Now he was calling me and saying he had a problem, and I felt like snapping back at him that I could match any of his problems ten times over.

"I need your help," he said.

*He needs* my *help*, I thought.

"We've voted to open up our church."

"Well, what do you mean?"

"We're opening our doors to Negro people."

"I still don't understand." I'm Presbyterian myself, and I couldn't imagine what he was talking about. Presbyterians are a righteous lot, but they don't move *that* fast.

"Mayor," he said, "it was unanimous. Our board of deacons voted on it and we're housing three hundred Negro citizens tonight. We'll provide meals for several thousands during the march when they pass by the church, and we'll have living quarters for as many as we can take. We're going to need six hundred blankets."

"Reverend Taylor," I said, "there's only one job bigger than my finding six hundred blankets, and that's your opening up your church to Negroes. You've got 'em."

So this was how Atlanta was going to react. In the back of my mind all along there had been great fears that the major factor in whether Atlanta was going to have serious trouble was not with the black people but the white racists who had always referred to Dr. King as "Martin Luther

Coon" and hated him and what he had done with an un-
swerving passion. I had received several telegrams and
phone calls from a surprisingly large number of these
people, and from some people I had respected in the past,
suggesting that the city ignore the funeral. Lester Maddox, of course, was cowering in the Capitol and making
an issue about the plan to lower flags in Atlanta to half-
mast, and there were rumors that he was going to call up
the National Guard for his personal protection. A mild
hysteria was running through the conservative community
and there was the possibility of still another assassination
with all of the liberal leaders descending on Atlanta at
one time. But here was a young Presbyterian minister
saying his church was opening its doors to Negro visitors.
Later in the day, hundreds of other white churches in the
city made similar announcements. Randy Taylor had
shown me the attitude Atlanta was going to take, and it
took only a minute to call Third Army headquarters and
get six hundred blankets.

Finally, on Monday morning, twenty-four hours before
the funeral was to take place, the big wheels began to
mesh. We knew by this time that Eastern Airlines was
going to have more charter flights coming into Atlanta
Monday and Tuesday than they had ever put into one
city in the history of the airline. We knew there were more
than forty Greyhound buses coming in from New York
City alone, with forty people to a bus. Then there were
the railroads and the private automobiles. It had taken us
four days to discover the magnitude of it, but now it appeared that more than one hundred thousand people
would be coming into Atlanta for the funeral. Not only
were the white and black churches of Atlanta opening
their doors to the visitors, but many private homes, black
and white, were also offering their rooms. Many of those
planning to come wouldn't have the means to rent hotel

rooms or dine at expensive restaurants; a lot of them just planned to come to Atlanta and worry about eating and sleeping when they got there. And then there would be the celebrities: the Kennedys, Harry Belafonte, Jacob Javits, John Lindsay, Wilt (The Stilt) Chamberlain, Jimmy Brown, James Brown, Nelson Rockefeller, Richard Nixon, Hubert Humphrey, and on and on and on. The crush was going to be fantastic.

All we could do was try to plan for every situation, every need, that might arise, and then hope for the best. When there is going to be, say, a huge sports event, plans are laid for weeks and months in advance. There are organizational meetings held, and everybody involved has ample time to prepare: hotels, restaurants, police, sanitation department, transportation facilities, etc. But we had been given only four full days to get ready, and our difficulties were compounded by the very real threat of violence. At a meeting with SCLC officials that day before the funeral, we assured them that the city would immediately issue purchase orders for such things as public-address systems and portable toilets along the line of march—and that we were prepared to foot the bill, no matter what the technicality might be over whether the funeral was public or private. We also finalized our security setup: in addition to the secret service and FBI and federal marshals, we would have fourteen hundred young Negro students serving as special marshals, plus five hundred uniformed city firemen and, for the first time in the city's history, every one of the thousand-plus employees of the Atlanta Police Department. We had done what we could. It was quiet again in Atlanta on Monday night as the population of the city began to swell and thousands of mourners inched through the darkness of the Morehouse College campus to take a last look at Martin Luther King, Jr.

Early on Tuesday morning, my wife and I went to the airport to meet some of the VIP's coming in for the funeral. There was John V. Lindsay and Nelson Rockefeller, who had come in on a chartered flight from New York City. Then, with Vice President and Mrs. Hubert Humphrey and Martin's brother A. D. King, we were driven as rapidly as possible to the Ebenezer Baptist Church where the funeral ceremony would be held—that same small church on Auburn Avenue where Dr. King, Sr., and his son had preached so many times.

When we reached the church there were perhaps one hundred thousand people in the immediate vicinity, all of them seemingly trying to get inside a church that could hold but eight hundred. It was a terrific crush. Squeals were going up on the sight of Jacqueline Kennedy or Jimmy Brown or Richard Nixon. The Secret Service was having a terrible time keeping the entrances clear so those invited to attend the service could get inside. Mrs. Allen and I were seated on the second row, directly behind the Vice President and his wife, and I was trying to see everything that went on. It was an anxious time for me. We could hear the jostling and wailing and yelling outside. I was talking to myself, pleading that nothing would go wrong. Many businesses had closed for the day, and there was a great deal of respect being shown for the memory of Martin Luther King. But, after all, this was the Old South. A good part of white Atlanta had stayed home. There was still great bitterness and opposition to the funeral. I could only hope that things would go as well outside as they were inside the church. The Negro ushers all wore morning coats and striped trousers, and they were somberly escorting all of these sad people down the aisles of the cramped and stuffy little church. Inside was the greatest galaxy of prominent national figures there had ever been in Atlanta at one time: Robert Kennedy, George

Romney, Mayor Carl Stokes of Cleveland, Nixon, Rockefeller, Harry Belafonte, and an endless array of others
equally as famous. Coretta King, sitting with her family
front and center in front of the casket, looked lovely and
courageous and dignified in a black mourning veil.

Once the service was completed, it was time for the
long procession to Morehouse College to begin. These
thousands of people would march along behind the mule-
drawn wagon carrying the body, would march down the
streets of Atlanta in the broiling sun, would march and
sing "We Shall Overcome," would march and dab at
their tear-streaked faces with handkerchiefs, would
march solemnly and respectfully in memory of a man
who had dedicated his life to the theory of nonviolent
protest in behalf of the dignity of man. There was going
to be no violence in Atlanta that day. In all of my ap-
prehensiveness I had failed to reckon with one great
factor: this entire mass of nearly two hundred thousand
mourners, every single one of them, was trying to honor
Martin Luther King, Jr., just as he had lived his life. Just
as he would have wanted it.

Except for the governor of Georgia, of course, who was
in his office behind drawn blinds and a cordon of some
hundred troopers. As the funeral procession slowly drew
past the Capitol, one reporter raced up the steps and into
the outer office and said he saw several of the governor's
aides peeking through the blinds and making jokes. "Yep,
caught the guy that did it and gave him five days in jail,"
one of them said. "For shooting 'coons out of season." I
remember glancing over toward the Capitol and thanking
God that I was on the side I was on, instead of on the
side of the racists who have plagued Georgia and the rest
of the South for more than one hundred years.

Although at least 46 people were killed in violence in

126 cities, there never *was* any trouble in Atlanta during those tense, traumatic days. But in the aftermath we had a chance to see just how close we might have come to yet another tragedy.

During the seating of the people inside Ebenezer Baptist Church, I had noticed that one of the men serving as an usher was entirely out of place. While the others were dressed in morning coats, this man—a wild-eyed white man—wore a bright yellow sport coat. He was right there inside the church, rushing up the aisle and showing prominent visitors like the Humphreys and the Romneys to their seats. He showed Louise and me to our seats. Then one of the black photographers in the pool of newsmen allowed to cover the ceremony left his group and challenged the white "usher." The photographer was angry. "What are you doing here?" he said. "You're a member of the Ku Klux Klan." The white man bristled, and they stood nose-to-nose for a few seconds until finally they parted. The white man took a seat in the same pew where we were, and in a few minutes Morris Redding decided to look into it. He sat down next to the man and introduced himself as being a visitor from Griffin, Georgia, and this way got the man's name. After the day had ended and we were driving back from the ceremony held at the end of the march on the Morehouse quadrangle (the man had been seen escorting Nelson Rockefeller and his party away from that, too, as though he were a personal bodyguard), we chuckled over the incident of the man in the yellow sport coat. Morris Redding promised me he would look it up and see if the man had a record, and that he would call me at home and give me a report.

It was some record, including several trips to insane asylums. This scared us to death. He hadn't done anything wrong, of course, even in playing usher at the church. But it was frightening to know that, in spite of all the heavy security, he had been able to slip right into the center of activity during the King funeral. Still, we had been lucky and nothing serious had happened and we were still grinning over the affair when we went to the opening game of the National League season that following Friday night at Atlanta Stadium. Louise and I were walking toward the Braves offices on the club-deck level, for a pregame cocktail party, when we saw Dr. King, Sr., being escorted by Lee Walburn of the Braves office staff and another man we didn't recognize. We thought it odd that he would be out at a Braves game so soon after his son's burial. We went over to them and chatted a few minutes, and noticed that Dr. King seemed highly disturbed. He said they were taking him over to the Stadium Club for dinner. And Louise and I walked on, and then she grabbed my arm and said, "Ivan, that was the man in the yellow sport coat."

I rushed into the Braves office and found pandemonium. They were wringing their hands, pacing back and forth. The man in the yellow sport coat had talked his way into the offices, with Dr. King in tow, and announced that he had brought Dr. King there to throw out the first ball. Actually, I was supposed to throw out the first ball that night. Dr. King then told how the man had come by his house and, against his will, told him he was supposed to be at the stadium for opening-night ceremonies and that he was supposed to take him there. I immediately called for Morris Redding, and eventually the man in the yellow sport coat was told in no uncertain terms that he should watch his step.

One week later, on network television, I saw where the same man had been snatched by the secret service trying to slip into the White House to talk to the President. He was put into a mental institution in Washington, the announcer said. I didn't know *what* to say.

# End of an Era

Since 1953, at least, Atlanta's mayors had been chosen by a coalition composed of virtually all black voters, most of the middle and upper-middle class whites who live on the northside of the city, and a minority of whites elsewhere . . . The previously successful coalition of blacks and northside whites was shattered in 1969 . . . Upper-middle class whites and the city's traditional "power structure" lost their former position of influence . . .

—*The Atlanta Elections of 1969,* a study by the Voter Education Project, Inc., Atlanta

Eight years was long enough in the mayor's office. We had charted our course and followed it with unparalleled success, and as we neared the end of the sixties I felt Atlanta had enough impetus to carry it into a new era without my hanging around. Although I am certain I could have been re-elected, possibly without any opposition, the commitment I had made in 1965 not to seek a third term was firm. I hadn't said anything about this commitment except to my wife and to Earl Landers, my administrative assistant, because it is a reality of politics

219

that you lose your influence and your power over the public and the people working under you if you don't leave the impression that you are a potential candidate for another term. In short, nobody wants to do business with a "lame-duck" mayor. But these things have a way of leaking out, no matter how careful you are to conceal them. In 1968 I began quietly passing the word in strictest confidence to some of the top leaders in the city, Jack Tarver, Eugene Patterson, Jack Spalding, Mills Lane, and Robert Woodruff, so they could begin thinking about a successor at City Hall. Inevitably, my plans to step down began to be whispered all over town. So, during the first week of January 1969—a full nine months before the mayoralty election—I formally announced my decision at a meeting of the Atlanta Rotary Club.

From that point on, I tried to make it clear at every opportunity that I intended to stay out of the race and make no public endorsement of any candidate. My primary reason for this was a feeling that my popularity with the voters of Atlanta was personal rather than political. I was one man, not the titular head of a political machine. My popularity had been built on what I had actually accomplished as mayor, rather than on patronage or political favors. I recognized that it would be unfair and probably futile for me to attempt to transfer this base to another candidate. So I repeatedly stated in private and in public that I would not publicly endorse any candidate, or otherwise inject myself into the race, so long as nothing was going wrong.

Almost immediately there were indications that times had changed; that this Atlanta mayoralty election was going to be like no other in the history of the city. A few days after my announcement at the Rotary Club I was visited by a delegation of Negro leaders including Dr. Martin Luther King, Sr., Jesse Hill, the Reverend Sam

Williams, and Senator Leroy Johnson. There were six or eight of them, the leading representatives of the black community, and they wanted simply to affirm their interest in continuing the traditional alliance between the white civic-and-business leadership and the black community. This, of course, was perfectly satisfactory to me. That coalition had always been responsible for selecting and then electing candidates in the city, especially me, both in 1961 and 1965. We had a general discussion about this for about two hours, and finally they asked me to serve as liaison man between the two groups so a satisfactory candidate for mayor could be found. This was perfectly proper—the logical, traditional way to go about it—and I agreed to their idea.

Less than a week later, however, the delegation called on me again. There had been no formal announcements for candidacy at that time, but it was almost certain that one of the candidates would be Alderman and State Representative Rodney Cook, a moderate white Republican who was in the insurance business, lived on the north side of town, and would hope to become the business community's man. To my shock, the black leaders flatly told me they would not accept Rodney Cook as a candidate under any circumstances. This was, I felt, a substantial deviation from the original plan. If the two groups were going to work together to select a candidate, how could one side come right out with a veto like that before there had been any discussion? There would have to be some give-and-take, but the black leaders were adamant in their position against Rodney Cook. After we talked about it awhile, it became apparent that there were some personal reasons involved (reasons still unclear to me) and that there was no way the black leadership of Atlanta would ever unite in behalf of Rodney Cook's candidacy. I told them that I didn't think this was an adequate way to start off our negotiations, and that I hoped they would reconsider.

Ironically, events clear across the nation—in Los Angeles —soon were to tear the roof off Atlanta's black community. In the mayoralty primary there, a black ex-policeman named Tom Bradley ran very strong against incumbent Sam Yorty. This, regardless of what anyone says, changed the entire attitude of the black electorate in Atlanta. Bradley's strong showing caused Atlanta's black leaders to feel they had made a mistake this time in wanting to work hand-in-hand as they always had with the "white power structure." For nearly two decades the black community had been a silent partner in the election of city officials in Atlanta, generally going along with whatever moderate candidate the white business and civic fathers endorsed. But they were quite aware of the fact that between 1961 and 1969 the proportion of blacks among the city's registered voters had increased from 29 per cent to nearly 41 per cent. And they also knew there was a much stronger Negro vote in Atlanta than in Los Angeles: 40 per cent, compared with only 25 per cent out there. If a Negro can make a showing like that in Los Angeles, they began to say to themselves, a Negro can be elected mayor of Atlanta. It was at this point that negotiations broke down between me and the black leadership of the city.

Perhaps it was inevitable that the black community would become divided within itself as soon as it had gained real strength for the first time in history. A fight for power promptly began between Senator Leroy Johnson, the first black state legislator in modern times, and Dr. Horace Tate of the all-black Georgia Teachers' Education Association. It was entirely inconsistent that these two men could fight each other in a power grab, both of them having fine records and believing in the same gen-

eral goals, but go to battle they did. Johnson craftily
stayed away from an official announcement of his candidacy until the Bradley-Yorty runoff in Los Angeles, but
Tate went ahead and jumped into the race. Everybody
was still waiting to see how the runoff in Los Angeles
would come out, with the clear understanding that if
Bradley knocked off Yorty there would be every possibility that a Negro might be elected mayor of Atlanta. It
didn't happen like that, of course. When it came to a nose-
to-nose confrontation between Bradley and Yorty at the
polls, white racism rose up to easily conquer the Negro
bloc vote and put Yorty back into office in a landslide.
With that, the Negro community in Atlanta split right up
the middle: half for Dr. Horace Tate, the city's first black
candidate for mayor; half for Sam Massell, the Jewish
realtor who had been my vice-mayor for all eight years.
Looking back, it is clear to me that Dr. Tate, an excellent
candidate who handled himself extremely well, could
have won, possibly without a runoff, if he had been able
to get the full support of Senator Leroy Johnson and the
Negro community.

Meanwhile, the situation was just as chaotic in the
white business community. It was known early in the year
that Sam Massell, Rodney Cook, and Everett Millican
—the latter a conservative "law-and-order" alderman—
would sooner or later get into the race. But in the beginning there was a feeling among the white civic leaders
that surely there must be a stronger candidate somewhere within their ranks, and for six or seven months there
were agonizing discussions of a number of possible candidates. As far back as January, right after my formal
declaration not to run for re-election, a poll showed that
one possibility would be Charles Weltner, the bright
young liberal Democrat who had given up his seat in Con-

gress as a protest against the election of Lester Maddox as governor of Georgia. It was perfectly obvious to me that the only white candidate in the city who could get enough of the black and liberal vote to beat Sam Massell would be Charlie Weltner, and I still think if we had been able to unite the business community in support of Weltner, he could have been elected. But there was some strong feeling that he was not a satisfactory candidate (Charlie was haunted by charges that he had "run out" on his constituents when he should have stuck it out and worked against the Maddox crowd "within the system"). Included among the other possible candidates we discussed were John Wilson, the incoming president of the Chamber of Commerce, Henry Bowden, the longtime city attorney, and any number of civic leaders such as Rawson Haverty, James Sibley, and Alex Smith.

In the end, the nod went to Rodney Cook. In July I called together a group of leading white citizens who were extremely interested in the race and gave them the results of a fairly thorough city-wide poll that had just been completed. The figures showed that Massell had 35 per cent of the vote, Cook 22 per cent, and Millican 16 per cent, with 27 per cent uncommitted. Breaking it down, the poll also showed that Massell had 52 per cent of the black vote, Cook 15 per cent, and Millican about 2 per cent, with 31 per cent not committed. This poll was taken, of course, before Dr. Horace Tate's entry into the race. At that meeting I told these 25 or 30 leaders of the white business and civic community that we should finance and support Rodney Cook wholeheartedly in an effort to force a runoff between Cook and Massell. Cook had a chance of winning, I said, if he could make at least *some* inroads in the black community and if he could pick up Millican's support in a runoff. The white business community only then finally united behind Rodney Cook for mayor, with the firm but reluctant understanding that he had only an outside chance.

Then Dr. Tate got into the race, dividing the black vote and giving us more hope. As we neared the October 7 election the picture seemed to be changing almost every day, with Tate becoming stronger as time went by. For example, about a month before the election a poll showed Massell with 28 per cent of the vote, Cook 23 per cent, Millican 20 per cent and Tate 19 per cent. Only *five days later,* in the last poll we took, we found that Tate had spurted up to 23 per cent, Massell and Millican were dropping off, and Cook was holding what he had. It was apparent that if this shift continued long enough from Massell to Tate, there could be a runoff between Tate and Massell or between Tate and Cook.

All along, the pressure became heavier on me to endorse Cook. Some people had the feeling that all I had to do was endorse him and the entire Negro community would support him, but I knew that was not the case. I knew the Negro leadership of Atlanta had finally broken away from the "white power structure" after all of those years, and that they would likely go for Massell in the end because they saw him as a candidate *they* could elect in a coalition with the Jewish people and the labor element and other minorities.

Personally, of course, I wanted to see Rodney Cook win. I was afraid Everett Millican would be too reactionary on the race issue. I felt Dr. Tate, as able an educator as he was, wouldn't be conversant enough with the political process to handle the job of mayor. And I simply didn't feel Sam Massell was qualified, although he was making inroads in the black community by implying he had been groomed for the job for eight years while serving under me as vice-mayor (in fact, the extent of the vice-mayor's duties in Atlanta is to serve as chairman at board-of-aldermen meetings and to represent City Hall at various functions when the mayor is absent).

Rodney Cook seemed to me to be the best of the four candidates: a northside businessman who had considerable experience in local government and had proved to be moderate on the race issue. Very early in the game, soon after my announcement not to run, I talked with each of the candidates several times and explained to them why I wanted to stay out of it publicly. I later supported Cook financially and personally, but not publicly. I steadfastly maintained the position, in six or seven group meetings and in private conversations throughout the summer, that I would not take a public stand on the race unless something went drastically wrong.

Then, about a month before the general election, I got a call from Police Chief Herbert Jenkins. In eight years he and I had been through a number of crises together, most of them racial, and we had developed complete confidence in, and loyalty to, each other. There was such rapport between us that he seldom called unless there were unusual circumstances. "Mr. Mayor," he said, "the vice-mayor has requested personal protection and I want to discuss the matter with you." We talked at length, about how there is always the danger of the police department being brought into politics and about how I had been faced with genuine physical threats against my family in 1961 but had *paid* for police protection. We agreed that times had changed, that Atlanta was a larger city now and there was a great deal more violence and fear in the air. "This is a request not only from a candidate but from the vice-mayor," I said, "and under these circumstances, Herbert, I would say to you that you have got to give him some type of personal protection. My recommendation is to furnish him complete protection, and if the other candidates want the same thing you must do the same for them. It'll put a drain on manpower, because this is a twenty-four-hour thing. But we've got to do it."

That was my recommendation, and I told Chief Jenkins to make his decision. Whatever his decision was, I would sustain him in it just as I always had. I figured that was the last I would hear of the matter.

But then, a day or two later, Jenkins called again and said, "Mayor, the problem is far more acute than I thought it was."

"What do you mean, 'acute'?"

"The vice-mayor wants a certain man on the force."

"I don't see anything wrong with that, Herbert."

"But he wants a captain."

"Good Lord," I said, "we've got more candidates than you've got captains. This is ridiculous. If the man wants protection, we'll give him an officer. But if the other candidates want help, they'll have to take patrolmen. Why does he want a captain, anyway?"

Jenkins said, "He wants a *specific* captain. Whalen."

"Why Whalen?"

"He says he knows him. He wants one he knows."

It was perplexing to me. "Herbert," I said, "It's unusual, but you've got the vice-mayor requesting this. If he wants Whalen and you can spare him, I recommend that you let him have him."

So Captain H. L. ("Buddy") Whalen, a native of Philadelphia who had risen quickly in the Atlanta Police Department in a dozen years, was assigned to give personal protection to Sam Massell. To our relief, none of the other candidates ever asked for protection. The incident was soon forgotten by me and the others who were closely watching the mayoralty race. October came, and then the general election on the seventh day of the month. Massell led with 31,000 votes (19,000 in the black precincts), followed by Cook with 27,000 (strong among northside whites), Tate with 23,000 (only 1,000 white votes), and Millican with 18,000 (only 1,000 black votes). The runoff two weeks later, on October 21, would pit Massell and Cook. There was still more pressure for me to come out and endorse Rodney Cook, but I continued to refuse to get into it publicly. Instead, I went on television and, calling the low turnout of only 46.5 per cent of the city's registered voters a "disgrace," appealed for civic and business groups to participate in "Operation Vote." It was simply an attempt to increase the turnout in the runoff election by organizing a telephone campaign and offering transportation to the polls, but immediately my appeal was branded by Massell's supporters as a veiled request for white voters to come out and vote against their candidate. I was beginning to get caught in the middle of a bitter fight, mostly because I still wouldn't endorse my choice for mayor.

Meanwhile, rumors started flying around town about how Massell had been misusing the police officer who had been assigned for his protection. What had happened was, as soon as Captain Whalen reported to Sam Massell's campaign headquarters in downtown Atlanta he was told that he would be working out of Massell's brother's office instead. That was on September 9. In the next ten days or so, Captain Whalen accompanied Howard Massell, a rather flamboyant man who lived in a showy home featuring a ceiling mirror in the bedroom, to various night clubs. At most of the clubs, Howard Massell talked to the owners or managers about contributing to his brother's campaign. He was doing this in the presence of a former vice-squad captain who was well known by most people in the Atlanta entertainment business. On September 20, Whalen went to his superiors and asked to be re-lieved of his assignment because he thought Howard Massell was "using my name and reputation in soliciting funds for his brother's campaign." Whalen was replaced on the assignment by a detective who was ordered to report daily to Whalen or his immediate superior, Superintendent of Detectives Clinton Chafin.

Chief Jenkins naturally found out about this situation as it developed, but he didn't report back to me. For one thing, our relationship had always been such that I had confidence in his ability and his integrity to do whatever was necessary in his department without having to come running to me every time a problem came up. And for another, Whalen didn't give his superiors the full story in the beginning. Based on what they knew at the time, Jenkins and Chafin moved properly and expeditiously— relieving Whalen and making it clear that his replacement was for Sam Massell's *personal protection* and nothing else—and there was no reason why they should have informed me of their actions. I bore no criticism of Chief Jenkins' actions. At that point they had only half-truths from Whalen, and it didn't seem necessary to investigate.

But then the story broke in the papers, less than a week before the runoff between Massell and Cook, and when that happened I immediately called for a complete investigation of the case. I asked for the investigation on the Thursday before the Tuesday runoff election. Whalen had left town to visit a brother in Philadelphia, and I asked Jenkins to bring him back to Atlanta and get a full report and submit it to me as quickly as possible. I left Atlanta on Saturday morning to spend the day with my son at Denison University in Granville, Ohio, on a special "fathers' day," and when I returned that night Chief Jenkins had a full report waiting for me.

Superintendent Chafin outlined what had happened at his end:

On or about September 9, on returning to my office from an outside appointment, I was informed by Captain H. L. Whalen that Chief Jenkins had advised him that he had received a call from Mr. Sam Massell and that Mr. Massell was receiving threats and wanted this department to furnish him a full-time guard . . .

I immediately called Mr. Sam Massell at the Allan-Grayson Company [and he] advised me that he thought it was necessary that he have a full-time man assigned to him and he would like for this man to be Captain H. L. Whalen.

I then advised Mr. Massell that Captain Whalen was working a special detail, investigating numerous shotgun shootings that had occurred in this city. He stated that he knew Buddy Whalen and that he wanted him, and I advised Captain Whalen to contact Mr. Massell and work this problem out . . .

Captain Whalen contacted me on September 20, and stated he had to talk to me, and that he had not been able to sleep due to some things that were happening on his present assignment . . .

Superintendent Chafin's report was followed by a detailed three-page typewritten report from Captain Whalen:

I reported to Mr. Massell on or about September 9, at his headquarters at the Dinkler Plaza Hotel, at that time Mr. Massell gave me some instructions and introduced me to his personnel working in the headquarters and told me of his itinerary for that date and the next day, that I should check his other campaign headquarters located in other sections of the city.

I was instructed by Mr. Sam Massell that I should work out of Mr. Howard Massell's office located at 30 Auburn Avenue, he stated that I should assist and work with Mr. Howard Massell when I was not working with him, that when he, Mr. Sam Massell needed me, he would know how to reach me through his brother, Howard Massell . . .

During the time that I was assigned to Mr. Massell I accompanied Mr. Howard Massell a couple of nights after we left the headquarters at the Dinkler Plaza. The nights that I accompanied Mr. Howard Massell, he went to [10 separate night clubs and strip joints] and at some of these locations, Mr. Howard Massell did talk with the owner or manager about a contribution for the campaign of his brother, Mr. Sam Massell. At no time did I solicit or have any conversation with anyone about the election or contributions nor did I receive any contributions from anyone . . .

I was stunned and indignant, as was Chief Jenkins. "The City of Atlanta has been free from this kind of activity for the last twenty-five years," he wrote in the report "and it cannot be tolerated in the future." I didn't approve of collecting campaign funds from night clubs in any manner, because this left you open to charges that you were beholden to the underworld. But collecting funds in this manner was more than that. It involved the blatant misuse of the police department. Anybody could get a license for a routine business in Atlanta, but to open a night club you were at the mercy of the police department: you were fingerprinted, your background was checked, and you were under constant surveillance. Here was the brother of a candidate asking the vulnerable night-club operator for a campaign contribution, in the presence of the former head of the vice squad, the implication being if the operator didn't come across and Sam Massell was elected there would be hell to pay. I had doubted all along whether Sam Massell would make a good mayor, and now I found him guilty of mishandling the power he already had as vice-mayor. There was no doubt in my mind, that Saturday night, less than seventy-two hours before the polls would open, that something *had* gone wrong and that I would have to take drastic action.

The next morning I called together four of my close

personal friends and asked them to read the complete
police report. All of us agreed that I should make a very
definite public statement and release the information in
the reports, in order to confirm the newspaper stories that
had been written and to absolve the police department of
any guilt. This, of course, would point the finger squarely
at Sam Massell. We recognized that Massell was ahead in
the race, and we knew that whatever I might say would
have little if any effect on the outcome. But I felt
very strongly that I had an obligation to speak out, just
as I had done so many times during my stay in office. I
had lashed out at Lester Maddox during the race in
1961. I had spoken out in behalf of public accommodations in the Senate. I had spoken out for reason during
the Summerhill riot. I had spoken out against Maddox's
nomination for governor. This was the posture I had assumed as mayor. I had never worried about losing personal popularity before, and there was no need to start
thinking about that now. I didn't think we could, at this
late date, get the public to understand the seriousness of
the charge against Massell. And certainly if Massell went
on to win, the Cook supporters would blame me for Rodney's defeat and the Massell people (meaning Helen Bullard, Dr. King, Sr., and so many others who had been
closely associated with me) would move farther away
from me. I had everything to lose and very little to gain
except my own peace of mind. Maybe that was enough.

That Sunday afternoon I called a press conference and
let the chips fall:

. . . It is my personal feeling that it is the vice-mayor rather
than his brother or Captain Whalen whose judgment is in question in this sorry situation.

Moreover, it is my considered conviction that the vice-mayor
has badly misused his position and that, if he is a man of con-
science, he should immediately withdraw from consideration for

an office which requires intuitive integrity and instinctive with-
drawal from even the suspicion and appearance of evil.

Officially, however, I am merely requesting that the news
media delineate the facts as fully as possible. And that, specifically, the *Atlanta Constitution* carry the complete text of Chief
Jenkins' report in tomorrow morning's edition so the voters
may read and finally evaluate the candidates for themselves.

The facts are such that, if all the voters fully understand, I
have complete confidence in their decision.

Understandably, my statement caused an uproar in
most parts of the city. Sam Massell and some of his people
were watching the press conference on a monitor at a
television station, where he was preparing for an election-
eve telecast, and reporters who were there said Mrs. Massell yelled "anti-Semitic" when I asked Sam to withdraw
from the race. The people on Rodney Cook's campaign
staff began saying bitterly and in private that I had just
lost the race for Rodney. The politicians around the city
and state were saying I had made a grievous error; that
I should have kept my mouth shut. The blacks and the
ultra-liberals were branding me as a traitor to their cause.
All I could do was hang in there and withstand the storm,
secure in the feeling that, just as on those many other occasions when I had taken a strong but unpopular stand,
I had spoken out for what I thought was right. Anti-
Semitic? I couldn't rationally be charged with anti-Sem-
itism after what I had done over the years in trying to
correct social injustices in Atlanta and the South. Grievous
political mistake? I never had been a politician, nor both-
ered myself with possible political repercussions, nor as-
pired to be "popular." Defeat Cook? We believed in our
polls and knew what was going to happen on election
day: Tate's votes had already polarized to Massell, Millican's to Cook, and it was too late to change that. Traitor
to the cause of the liberals and blacks? Impossible, after

a career devoted to their causes; there is nobody in the world more violent than an ultra-liberal when he gets caught sucking eggs in the henhouse, which is precisely what had happened. Vengeance against Sam Massell? Had my candidate, Rodney Cook, been involved in the same affair I am convinced I would have taken the same action—except that, if I had it to do all over again, I would have gone into greater detail to make the public fully understand the seriousness of the situation.

The vote went exactly as we had been expecting. WAGA-TV ran public opinion surveys on Monday, the day before the election, and they showed there was only a slight shift to *Cook* following my charge—so slight that it could be called no change at all. Massell picked up Tate's black supporters in the runoff, and Cook got Millican's conservative white support, and the totals gave Massell 55 per cent of the city-wide vote. Breaking it down, it was clear that a new coalition—labor, liberals, blacks—had won this mayoralty race (Massell received 45,000 black and 17,500 white votes, Cook 3,800 black and 47,500 white). This new coalition was also effective in most of the other races. Maynard Jackson, a well-bred and intelligent young Negro attorney, defeated respected white Alderman Milton Farris on the first ballot with 58.2 per cent of the total vote to make him the first black vice-mayor in the city's history (even the white business community had agreed that it was time to acknowledge the Negro's growing influence in Atlanta by supporting Jackson as vice-mayor). Black representation on the board of aldermen jumped from one to five, out of a possible eighteen. The number of Negroes on the ten-member board of education rose from two to three (Dr. Horace Tate later being named chairman by Massell). It wasn't a black "takeover" by any means, as many of the more paranoid reactionaries in Atlanta were saying. Blacks now occupied thirty per cent of the elective offices in a city where they comprised forty-nine per cent of the population. But times had changed, most abruptly and most certainly.

There were scars, of course, as there always are after a bitterly fought election. I immediately went to Sam Massell on election night, congratulating him on television and pledging my full cooperation, but it was obvious that I would not be accorded any special privileges at City Hall, nor did I ask for them. The position I had taken during the campaign caused me to lose some of my standing in the liberal and black communities, which I reluctantly accepted as a bitter fact of political life. I was only interested in seeing that Atlanta did not totally lose its perspective as it moved into a new era at City Hall. I tried to hammer home that point as I stood before the board of aldermen on the night of Sam Massell's inauguration as the new mayor and delivered what amounted to my farewell address:

When I stood here eight years ago and assumed the office of mayor, Atlanta was an outstanding regional city seeking her place in the sun, but had not yet come to grips with the anguish and the challenge of modern urban society. The ingredients for success were present in our natural, our economic and our human resources, and when these came together in determination to move this city forward, the momentum really began . . .

The degree of physical change in Atlanta during the past eight years has been without equal in the nation. By all growth indices, Atlanta has been the nation's "city of the sixties." But the greatest change in Atlanta has not been measured in skyscrapers and bank clearings. The real story of our progress during the decade has been Atlanta's reevaluation of human values, and our dedication to social improvement and equality . . .

Atlanta has consistently moved ahead of the tide of social

change. In public accommodations, in school desegregation, in voting rights, in housing, and in employment—we have surpassed every other city in America in real achievement. The ability of our people to accept the social change that has marked the urban crisis of this decade transcends even our capacity for unexecelled material growth . . .

Atlanta is unique. I cannot really define its uniqueness or give it a name. But I have lived it, and so has each one of you. Can Atlanta retain her uniqueness? Amid the gloss of great success, with the pressures of changing patterns, can she keep her balance? There is danger that bigness for its own sake will override our human values. There is also the danger that in our quest for human values we will erode our economic base which gives stability to those values.

In Atlanta's quest for continued greatness and social change, one principle must be kept before the people of the city and the new governmental leaders: The greatest threat to combatting poverty, to instituting social improvements, is a declining local economy. It is one thing to advance the underemployed to a livable wage when good jobs are available, but quite another when work is scarce. Providing adequate housing to replace the city's slums is an achievable goal when economy is on the upswing, but out of the question when there is no money for development.

Social improvement cannot take place in a vacuum, or during a time of economic recession. The key is balance. Atlanta must continue to produce more jobs, a growing tax base, cultural and athletic activities, a profitable business environment, and pride in the community. To neglect these factors in favor of putting all emphasis on social improvement only retards that very improvement . . .

# Epilogue

I wouldn't be discouraged, Ivan. You gave Atlanta enough momentum to carry it for another twenty-five years, no matter who's in City Hall.

—Eugene Patterson,
former editor of
the *Atlanta Constitution*

And so it was over. I wasn't especially crestfallen or surprised to find myself not so popular in some circles in the aftermath of Sam Massell's election, because I had become immune to criticism a long time before that. From the very beginning I had made up my mind that I was going to be totally independent, that I was going to do only what I thought was best for my city, that if I was going to run Atlanta and run it right I would have to put aside any political ambitions that might influence my decisions from City Hall. That is why I condemned Les-

ter Maddox, testified in behalf of John F. Kennedy's public-accommodations bill, asked Sam Massell to get out of
the mayor's race, and took any number of other actions
that I might not have taken if I had been interested in
furthering a political career. That is why I turned down
an opportunity to go to Washington around 1965 and
serve as a national director of community relations under
the Johnson Administration; and why I turned down an
offer from the Nixon Administration in 1969 to become
national director of urban affairs. All I ever wanted, after
my brief attempt at running for governor of Georgia, was
to be a good mayor of Atlanta. To hell with the critics.
I had done my best, and I could sleep well at night, so
when I gave way to Massell I went back to the Ivan Allen
Company. In many ways it seemed I was busier now
than when I was mayor. I had my normal executive duties
at my own company, was on the board of several corporations such as Cox Broadcasting and Southern Airways,
and in the summer of 1970 I was named chairman of a
Ford Foundation-sponsored commission studying police
departments. In the first few months I had precious little
contact with city government or with most of those who
had been enraged by my "attack" on Massell, although
there were indications that they would begin to come
around once the heat of battle subsided.

To say the bubble had burst would be too poetic. But
there was a great deal of frustration within the business
community as the decade ended. Suddenly we were regarded in certain circles as evil men—the "white power
structure" was a term used with more bite now than ever
before—who had never made a move unless it promised
to be beneficial to our own personal desires. Our efforts
in coping with the racial crisis were dismissed on grounds
that we weren't really "sincere" in wanting to help the
Negro secure his rights. Our outstanding record of physi-

cal growth merely brought us charges that we had an "edifice complex" and cared more about urban renewal than about "human renewal." Gleefully, our critics pictured us as a government-in-exile: petulant, sulking behind our mahogany desks, tails between our legs, crying because after all these years we had failed once to have things our own way. The argument I had made for several years that Atlanta had to broaden its tax base by bringing the upper-class white suburbs into the city was now being branded as an attempt to dilute the vote of the Negro, who would soon have 50 per cent of the vote. It was even suggested that the Forward Atlanta program, by bringing in more people and fresh industry, had been a curse rather than a blessing: creating problems in pollution, housing, and transportation. The transition from the sixties to the seventies was not the best of times for Atlanta's "white power structure."

Yet, I submit that no major city in America has ever been guided by a group of men who were so totally dedicated—*albeit*, pragmatically, benevolently, and paternalistically—to the welfare and prosperity of *their* city. That was the secret to Atlanta's success in the sixties. When I look back at what happened during the decade I can find few major efforts that were accomplished without the totally unselfish support of the business community.

Banker Mills Lane got the stadium project rolling. Realtor Jack Adair developed the Atlanta Civic Center. Editor Eugene Patterson urged racial understanding, and publisher Jack Tarver gave advice. Banker Ed Smith made it possible for my second bond issue to be understood by the public and, as a result, passed. Robert Woodruff of Coca-Cola endorsed, with anonymous gifts, nearly every critical fund-raising drive to come up. Architect Cecil Alexander ran the housing resources department for the city. Bank board chairmen Jack Glenn and George Craft were responsible for seeing that more low-income housing was built during my eight years than in the entire thirty years prior to that. It was Boisfeuillet Jones of the Woodruff Foundation and bank president Billy Sterne who made Economic Opportunity Atlanta the strongest antipoverty program in America. It was Arthur Montgomery who kept punching until he got a major-league baseball team. It was Leonard Reinsch who was responsible, in the end, for bringing big-league professional football to the city. It was department-store executive Dick Rich who spearheaded the attempts at rapid transit. And it was young Tom Cousins, who, caught up in the fervor of the older business community dedication, went out and brought the Hawks to Atlanta.

The list is endless. In every case, all I had to do was suggest that Atlanta had a need, ask a member of the "power structure" to look after it, and merely sit back and wait until it was done. The sixties was the right time, Atlanta was the right city, and this business community was the right one. No city had ever seen anything like it before, and no city is likely to see it again.

Whether we were "sincerely liberal" is inconsequential. We succeeded in Atlanta because we were realistic. We established a logical game plan in the beginning— basically, the Six-Point Program—and we followed it. Coping with the racial issue and making long-range plans were the keys. When the racial problem was reasonably settled, it cleared the way for everything else: new industry, expressways, sports, jobs, entertainment, housing. One begets another, in a fascinating chain of events. When you "solved" your racial problems, you earned a favorable national image. A favorable image attracts new industry. New industry means more jobs. More jobs mean more personal income and spending. More income and spending mean a broader tax base for the city, which means more and better city services, which mean happier people, which is what it is all about. It is wonderful to be idealistic and to speak about human values, but you are not going to be able to do one thing about them if you are not economically strong. If there is any one slogan I lived by as mayor of Atlanta, that would be it.

On my last day in office I was up to here in nostalgia. Arrayed around my desk were the eight Kennedy rockers, and I could remember the day Morris Abram sat in one and told me President Kennedy wanted me to testify in Washington. On the walls hung the gold souvenir shovels signifying various important groundbreaking ceremonies. Here was my own personal Atlanta Braves cap. There was a map showing the Model Cities project area, which included Summerhill. And out the window there were the Civil War cannons on the lawn of the Capitol, behind which Lester Maddox still hid.

I spent much of the day reminiscing about the eight years that were coming to an end, and calling to thank those who had been at my side. One of those I called was Eugene Patterson, who had left the *Constitution* to become managing editor of the *Washington Post*.

"How do you feel?" he said.

"Tired," I told him.

"No, I mean about the election."

"Discouraged. I don't know what to expect."

"I wouldn't be discouraged, Ivan," he said. "You gave Atlanta enough momentum to carry it for another twenty-five years, no matter who's in City Hall."

I said, "I can't say I agree with you."

"Well, it's true."

"But I appreciate the thought."

# Index

243